ABU SIMBEL
ASWAN
and the
NUBIAN TEMPLES

WHITE STAR
PUBLISHERS

1 RAMESSES II, ARMED WITH BOW AND ARROW, MOVES TO ATTACK A SYRIAN FORTRESS WITH HIS WAR CHARIOT.

2-3 THE FAÇADE OF THE GREAT TEMPLE OF ABU SIMBEL IS DOMINATED BY FOUR, NEARLY 70-FOOT-TALL COLOSSI OF RAMESSES II.

4-5 IN 1964, THE TEMPLE OF WADI ES-SEBUA WAS MOVED ABOUT TWO-AND-A-HALF MILES WEST OF ITS ORIGINAL POSITION.

6 NEFERTARI, WITH THE TYPICAL HATHORIC HEAD COVERING, HOLDS A SISTRUM IN HER RIGHT HAND AND AN OFFERING OF FLOWERS IN HER LEFT.

7 ROSELLINI'S DRAWING RECREATES THE PHARAOH'S CEREMONIAL CHARIOT THAT APPEARS IN THE RELIEF OF QADESH IN THE RAMESSEUM.

8-9 COMMERCIAL RIVER TRAFFIC WAS MONITORED FROM ELEPHANTINE ISLAND, SITUATED AT THE SOUTHERN BORDER OF EGYPT.

10-11 THE FIRST PYLON OF THE TEMPLE AT PHILAE, THE WORK OF PTOLEMY XII, BEARS CEREMONIAL SCENES IN WHICH THE SOVEREIGN MASSACRES HIS ENEMIES AND MAKES OFFERINGS TO THE ANCIENT EGYPTIAN GODS.

12-13 THE NILE RIVER, AT THE SOUTHERN BORDER OF EGYPT, IS SEEN HERE FROM THE DESERT, CLOSE TO ASWAN.

TEXT
MARCO ZECCHI

GRAPHIC DESIGN
MARIA CUCCHI

EDITORIAL COORDINATION
LAURA ACCOMAZZO

© 2004 White Star S.r.l.
Via C. Sassone, 22/24
13100 Vercelli, Italy - www.whitestar.it

TRANSLATION
AMY CHRISTINE EZRIN

ISBN 88-544-0016-5

REPRINTS:
1 2 3 4 5 6   08 07 06 05 04

Printed in Thailand by Sirivatana
Color separation by Chiaroscuro, Turin

CONTENTS

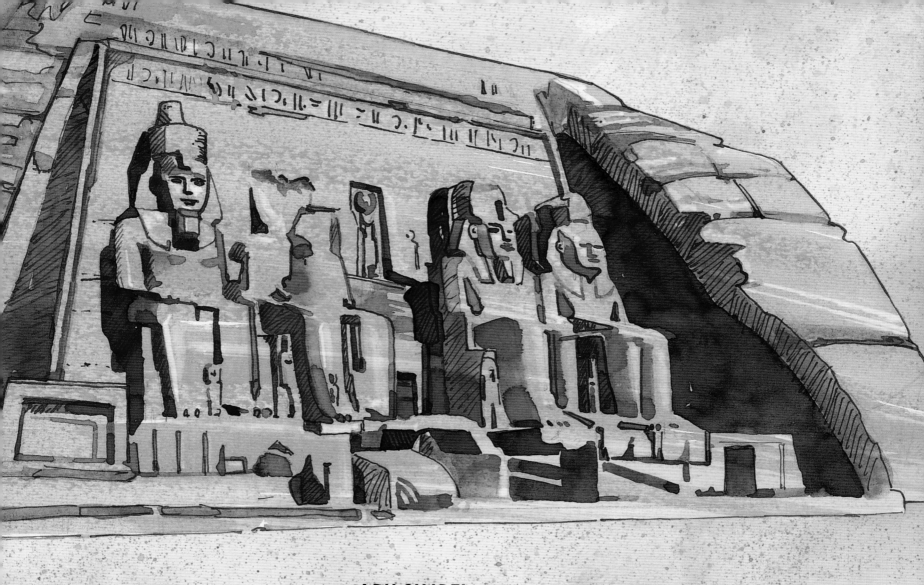

ABU SIMBEL
GREAT TEMPLE

AL-MAHARRAQA

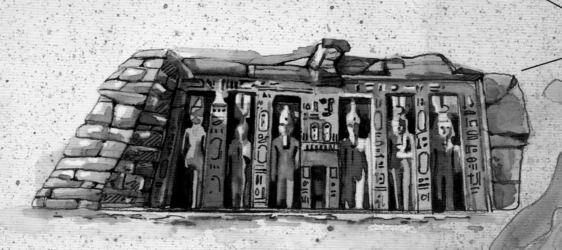

ABU SIMBEL
SMALL TEMPLE

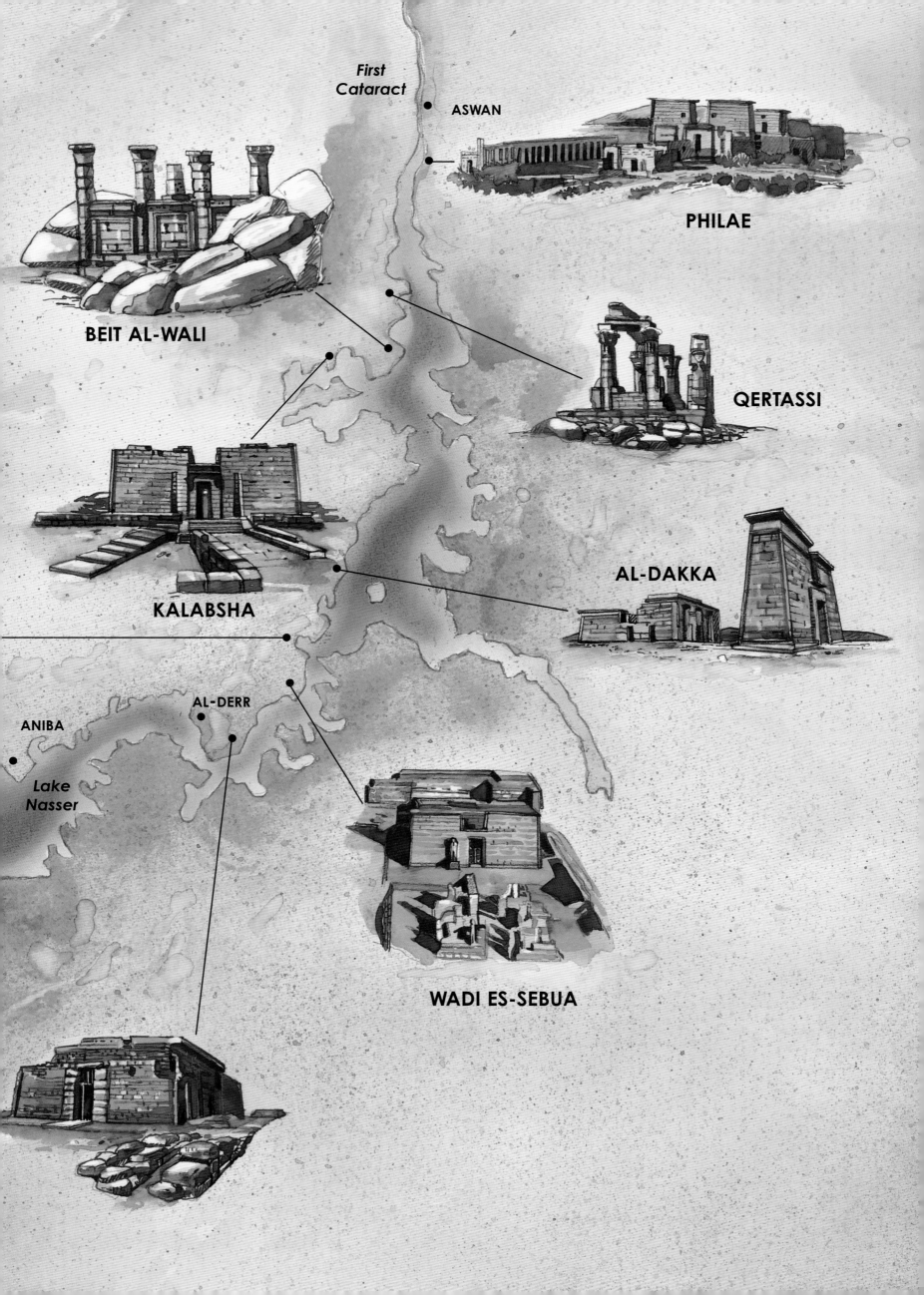

First
Cataract

ASWAN

PHILAE

BEIT AL-WALI

QERTASSI

AL-DAKKA

KALABSHA

AL-DERR

ANIBA

Lake
Nasser

WADI ES-SEBUA

NUBIA

Nubia is a vast geographical area that begins south of Aswan and ends at the confluence of the White Nile and the Blue Nile, at the point where Khartoum, the capital of the Sudan, now stands. This region extends for almost 3,300 miles as the crow flies but for about double that distance it follows the course of the Nile, which differs somewhat from the Nile that runs through Egypt. In Nubia, the river's fall is greater and is marked at intervals by rapids, which geographers have named 'cataracts' and which have been numbered from the north (First Cataract) to the south (Sixth Cataract). Originally, the area of Elephantine Island and Aswan was Nubian territory, and later, still in ancient times, it was incorporated into Upper Egypt and the border between the two countries was formally set at the First Cataract.

Like Egypt, which was divided into Upper and Lower Egypt, Nubia was also subdivided in two geographical areas. The region between the First Cataract (just a bit south of Aswan) and the Second Cataract was the so-called Lower Nubia, named Wawat by the ancient Egyptians, and is the area discussed in this volume. South of the Third Cataract, Upper Nubia begins, which the Ancient Egyptians called the Land of Kush. Since ancient times, the Egyptians had sought to extend their influence over Nubia. As a matter of fact, this region, besides constituting a sort of 'buffer' along Upper Egypt's southern frontier, was important for commerce and cultural exchanges with the African world. Moreover, the region offered gold, minerals, lumber, and exotic products, in addition to men employable in the Egyptian army. Under the earliest dynasties, the Egyptians began to exploit Nubia, periodically raiding it to procure livestock and capture prisoners. Under the First Dynasty (ca. 3100-2700 B.C.), the armed forces of Pharaoh Djer reached the Second Cataract. During the Old Kingdom (ca. 2700-2184 B.C.), the Egyptians passed the Second Cataract and intensified commercial relations, resorting also the use of force. In the Middle Kingdom (ca. 2040-1782 B.C.), the Egyptians subjected Nubia to military control as far as the Second Cataract. This occupation was facilitated by the construction of a series of forts in strategic positions in the region and allowed for the commercial colonization of the area. With Pharaoh Senusret III (ca. 1878-1841 B.C.) of the Twelfth Dynasty, the systematic exploitation of the conquered territory was organized. At Kerma, beyond the Third Cataract, a permanent commercial company was established. During the Second Intermediate Period (ca. 1782-1570 B.C.), Nubia enjoyed a period of independence, but in the New Kingdom (ca. 1570-1070 B.C.) under the leadership of the Eighteenth Dynasty pharaoh Thutmosis III (ca. 1504-1450 B.C.), the Egyptian army reached as far south as the Fourth Cataract. Nubia was then governed by an autonomous administration directed by the Viceroy of Nubia, who bore the title of 'Royal Son of Kush.' In this period in Lower Nubia, numerous temples were built, many of which date to the reign of Ramesses II (ca. 1278-1212 B.C.) of the Nineteenth Dynasty. During the New Kingdom, Egyptian superiority was at its height, but this did not prevent a reversal of roles from occurring in the not too distant future.

NUBIA

Since the Old Kingdom, the pharaohs of Egypt employed Nubians in their army; in particular, they formed a division of the police, the Medjai. The Nubians came to be civilized by the Egyptians to the point of adopting their beliefs, writing methods, and customs; at the same time, however, they began to realize their own importance and strength. Then, at the end of the Third Intermediate Period (664-332 B.C.), a Nubian dynasty from Napata, situated between the Third and Fourth cataracts, occupied Egypt, creating the Twenty-fifth Dynasty in Egypt. These pharaohs, whose names (e.g., Shabaka, Shabataka, Taharqa, Tantamani) betray their non-Egyptian origins, imposed their domination for about a century (750-664 B.C.), also making sure to present themselves and act like legitimate pharaohs in all ways. Nonetheless, after being defeated by the Assyrians, they returned to their home area around the Fourth Cataract. Defeated by Pharaoh Psammetichus (Psamtik) II (595-589 B.C.) of the Twenty-sixth Dynasty, the Nubians stopped involving themselves in Egyptians affairs and created their own indigenous culture (the Meroitic culture, named after the city of Meroë), whose total duration lasted for a full 1,200 years. The long existence of the kingdom of Kush is divided into two phases, named after the capitals of the time: that of the kingdom of Napata and that of the kingdom of Meroë (between the Fifth and Fourth Sixth Cataracts).

For a few years, both Meroitic culture and also Egyptian culture of the Ptolemaic and early Roman period simultaneously influenced Nubia. In this era, in Lower Nubia, temples in honor of Egyptian divinities were again built.

16 *LAKE NASSER EXTENDS FOR ABOUT 310 MILES AND IS ABOUT 300 FEET DEEP.*

17 *THE NILE AND LAKE NASSER ARE SURROUNDED BY DESERT.*

18-19 *A SATELLITE REVEALS THE INDENTED SHORES OF LAKE NASSER.*

19 *THE CREATION OF LAKE NASSER LED TO THE DISAPPEARANCE OF SEVERAL SITES.*

NUBIA

21 TOP THE DAM HAS LED TO THE LOSS OF TWO THIRDS OF THE ARABLE TERRITORY.

21 BOTTOM FOR THE ANCIENTS, NUBIA WAS THE WAY OF ACCESS TO THE HEART OF AFRICA.

20-21 LOWER NUBIA, AN OFTEN HARSH AND DESOLATE TERRITORY, EXTENDS FROM THE FIRST CATARACT, NEAR ASWAN, TO THE SECOND CATARACT.

20 BOTTOM A ROAD RUNS PARALLEL TO THE RIVER. AT TIMES, IT IS POSSIBLE TO ENCOUNTER BRIEF STRETCHES OF CULTIVATED LAND.

NUBIA

22 *The name Nubia was derived from 'Nuba,' the name of a population that immigrated there in the first to second century A.D.*

23 *top* *Lower Nubia is full of primary materials, especially gold, semi-precious stones, and incense.*

23 *bottom* *The Nubian landscape is often characterized by the desert that reaches up to the river.*

24-25 *In order to save it from the waters of Lake Nasser, the temple of Dakka was moved about 25 miles south of its original position.*

THE EXPLORATION

At the beginning of the nineteenth century, very few of the Europeans traveling in Egypt and who had sailed up the Nile had gone past Philae Island and none had ever ventured beyond al-Derr, the capital of Lower Nubia at the time. The first European to venture into Nubia may have been the Danish traveler Frederick Norden, between 1737-38. In any case, Norden never left the boat on which he was traveling, limiting himself to observing the Nubian monuments from afar by telescope. In addition, he gave up trying to sail up the Nile beyond al-Derr.

Years later, in 1813, the Swiss Johann Ludwig Burckhardt introduced himself to the governor of al-Derr under the name of Ibrahim Ibn Abdallah and, in exchange for a few gifts, succeeded in getting permission to continue his travels in Nubia. On March 2, 1813, accompanied by only a guide, Burckhardt began his journey toward a region in which no European had ever set foot. On the back of a camel, he skirted the Second Cataract and got as far as Dongola, describing the geography and antiquities of the region.

OF NUBIA

26-27 The temple of Dendur has been reproduced here by Rifaud, the sculptor who worked with Drovetti in his research of ancient objects.

27 top F. Norden was a navy officer sent to Egypt by the king of Denmark, Christian VI.

27 center This drawing of the temple of Dakka is the work of Rifaud, a sculptor from Marseille who lived in Egypt for about 40 years.

27 bottom Drovetti was a retired colonel of the French army in Egypt.

Upon returning to Dongola on March 22, Burckhardt decided to make a visit to Abu Simbel, then called Ibsambul, in order to visit the small temple, of which he described the façade and the interior. Then, suddenly, after having followed a very steep canyon, the big temple, at the time unknown, appeared to him. These were his words, "… by happy chance I walked a few steps away towards the south and my eyes met the still visible part of four immense colossal statues, cut into the rock … it is truly a shame that they are almost completely buried in the sand." Burckhardt can therefore be considered the modern discoverer of the big temple at Abu Simbel.

In 1815, with the advice of Burchardt himself, William Bankes, a rich Englishman in search of adventure, reached Abu Simbel. After him, in March 1816, Bernardino Drovetti, who had just resigned his post as France's consul-general in Egypt visited the place. Like Burckhardt, Drovetti could see only the upper part of the big temple, which arose above the sand.

28-29 IN SEPTEMBER 1816,
BELZONI STOPPED HIS BOAT IN
FRONT OF ABU SIMBEL, WHERE HE
DREW THIS DRAWING.

28 BOTTOM THE DRAWING OF
THE FIRST ATRIUM WITH OSIRID
PILLARS IN THE TEMPLE OF ABU
SIMBEL WAS THE WORK OF
BELZONI.

29 TOP GIAN BATTISTA BELZONI
(1778-1823) DISCOVERED THE
TOMB OF SETI I IN THE VALLEY OF
THE KINGS AND WAS THE FIRST TO
GAIN ACCESS INTO THE PYRAMID
OF KHAFRE.

29 BOTTOM BELZONI LEFT
BEHIND SOME WRITINGS FULL OF
ILLUSTRATIONS, LIKE THIS ONE
SHOWING A MOTIF TAKEN FROM
THE TEMPLE OF ABU SIMBEL.

The first European to set foot inside the big temple was the ex-circus strongman from Padua, Gian Battista Belzoni, who reached Abu Simbel on September 16, 1816 in the company of his wife Sarah. Belzoni was in the service of the British consul, Henry Salt, and he crossed Egypt and Nubia, bringing back precious monuments for the British Museum in London. As soon as he arrived at Abu Simbel, Belzoni tried to free the temple's façade from the sand, but in vain. Belzoni left the site after a few days, but was ready to return there in June 1817. This time Frederick William Beechey, Salt's secretary, and Charles Leonard Irby and James Mangles, two Royal Navy captains, were with him. The group set sail from Philae Island and reached the Second Cataract, returning downstream on July 4 in order to reach Abu Simbel. A few days later, with the help of some laborers, the sand-removal project got underway. Finally, on July 30, as night was about to fall, the upper part of the door appeared above the sand. Belzoni and his companions were able to create an opening by which to enter the temple, but they decided to explore it the next morning. At dawn, they met in front of the temple and entered the building. The group then explored and measured the temple in heat that reached 131°F or more.

Belzoni and his collaborators left Abu Simbel on August 4, carving their names and date of entry into the temple on a wall inside the sanctuary, thus commemorating their enterprise.

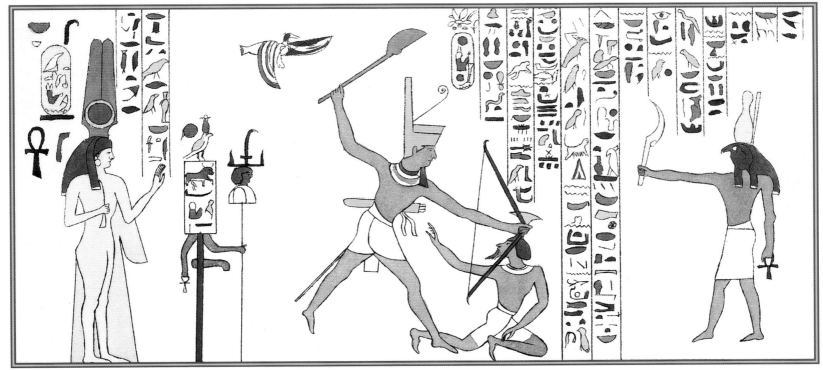

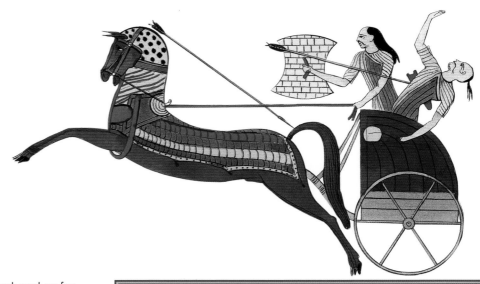

30 BOTTOM *THE RESULTS OF THE FRENCH-TUSCAN EXPEDITION WERE PUBLISHED BY CHAMPOLLION AND BY ROSELLINI (SHOWN HERE).*

30-31 TOP *IN THIS DRAWING COPIED FROM THE ONE DONE BY ROSELLINI AT ABU SIMBEL, THE EGYPTIANS CLOSE IN ON THE HITTITE CHARIOTS AT QADESH.*

30-31 BOTTOM *THE DRAWING DONE BY ROSELLINI SHOWS THE SELF-DEIFIED RAMESSES II IN FRONT OF AMUN-RA AND THE GODDESS MUT.*

After Belzoni, the number of those who ventured as far south as the Second Cataract grew. Nonetheless, the first scientific expedition to sail the Nile as far as Lower Nubia would have to wait for Jean-François Champollion, who had earlier used the Rosetta Stone in his quest to decipher hieroglyphics. This French-Tuscan expedition also included Ippolito Rosellini, an Orientalist from Pisa, in addition to other scholars. From December 26 to 28, 1828 and from January 3 to 16, 1829, the expedition was located near the temple of Abu Simbel, of which Champollion wrote, "It is such a wonder that it would be exceptional even at Thebes … a masterpiece worthy of all our admiration." The discoveries of this expedition, which pushed on as far as Wadi Halfa, were published between 1832 and 1844 in nine volumes of text and three of illustrated plates, titled *The Monuments of Egypt and Nubia.*

32 TOP THE DRAWING BY ROSELLINI REPRODUCES RAMESSES II KILLING A FOREIGN CHIEF WITH A LANCE AND TRAMPLING ANOTHER.

32 BOTTOM THE ANCIENT EGYPTIAN FORCES PIERCE THEIR ENEMIES BLOCKADED WITHIN A FORTRESS WITH ARROWS.

32-33 RAMESSES II, IN THE PRESENCE OF AMUN-RA, GRABS HIS ENEMIES BY THE HAIR BEFORE INFLICTING THE FATAL BLOW.

At this point, the almost fantastic feats of the first expeditions were finished. After the French-Tuscan expedition another one followed in 1831 organized by Robert Hay, the Earl of Tweedsdale, who laid the foundations of British Egyptology. Nonetheless, the first drawings and methodical and exhaustive description of the Nubian monuments was the work of the Prussian expedition led by Karl Richard Lepsius of Berlin. The members of this expedition met at Alexandria in September 1842. The following month they were in Thebes, from where they departed for Aswan and Nubia. In December of 1843, Lepsius and his team worked at the great temple of Abu Simbel; in nine days of hard labor they had copied the inscriptions and completed their surveys and measurements,

With the passage of time, travel in Nubia was no longer considered an undertaking full of danger, and Abu Simbel slowly became a destination for rich travelers. In 1845, J.J. Ampère, son of the great French physicist, visited all the Nubian temples, in the company of artist Paul Durand, as he sailed toward the Second Cataract. Unfortunately, Ampère never published the results of his trip to Egypt and Nubia. However, his journal demonstrates that he was aware of archeological issues. He made a very interesting study on the colors the ancient Egyptians chose for their hieroglyphics, "I noticed that the hieroglyphics that represent a part of the human body are red ... red is the color of the heart, receiver of the blood. Red, the color of fire, is attributed to all that which burns .... The hieroglyph for water is blue .... Yellow is the natural color of signs that relate to the light ...." However, the writer Gustave Flaubert should be remembered too for his diary entry. Having reached Abu Simbel with his friend Maxime DuCamp, he wrote, "Thought: the Egyptian temples bore me deeply."

The era of photography followed, which allowed for a greater and easier diffusion of the images of the Nubian monuments. On August 16, 1861, L.E. Méhédin took the first photograph of the interior of the hypostyle hall in the great temple at Abu Simbel.

a

b

THE EXPLORATION OF NUBIA

38-39 The photo shows a drawing by Lepsius of the first atrium of the big temple of Abu Simbel, with the Osirid pillars still partially covered by sand.

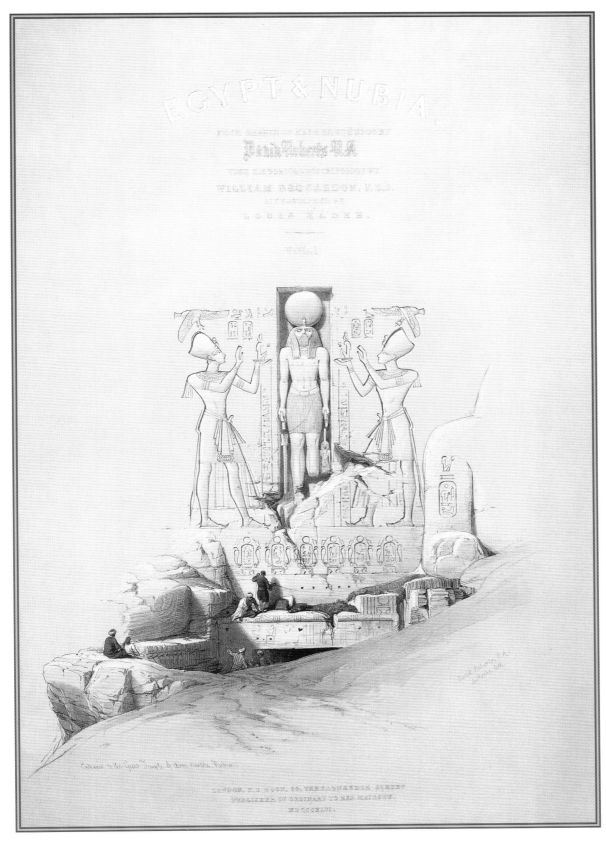

40 DAVID ROBERTS, SHOWN HERE IN ARAB CLOTHING, TRAVELED EXTENSIVELY IN EGYPT AND NUBIA.

41 LEFT THE FRONTISPIECE IN ONE OF ROBERTS' VOLUMES, THIS LITHOGRAPH ILLUSTRATES THE ENTRANCE TO THE GREAT TEMPLE.

41 RIGHT GASTON MASPERO (TOP) AND AUGUSTE MARIETTE WERE TWO OF THE MOST ILLUSTRIOUS EGYPTOLOGISTS OF THE NINETEENTH CENTURY.

42-43 AND 44-45 THE GREAT TEMPLE, PARTIALLY HIDDEN BY SAND, AND THE MAGNIFICENT TEMPLE OF PHILAE WERE RENDERED WITH GREAT SKILL BY ROBERTS.

August Mariette, the first director-general of the Egyptian Antiquities Service, never took much of an interest in Nubia. He placed neither inspectors nor research facilities there and barely succeeded in making an inspection of the area between Philae Island and the Second Cataract. The state of abandonment of the monuments of this region was considerable; however, between 1867 and 1870 the façade of the temple of Abu Simbel was almost completely cleared of sand.

From January 31 to February 18, the English journalist Amelia Blandford Edwards (recovering from a romantic disappointment), stopped at Abu Simbel with a group of friends. The trip in Egypt and Nubia gave a significant turn to her life. Upon returning to England, she dedicated herself to Egyptology with great enthusiasm. In 1877, she published a fine book, *A Thousand Miles up the Nile,* in which she described her voyage. In 1882, together with Reginald Stuart Poole and Erasmus Wilson, she founded an important scientific institute, the Egypt Exploration Foundation (today the Egypt Exploration Fund), becoming its first secretary. Moreover, she successfully fought to ensure that a department of Egyptology was created at the University College of London.

In 1881, Gaston Maspero succeeded Mariette. He paid more attention to the problems of the Nubian monuments. Unfortunately, between 1881 and 1885, because of the war unleashed by the Mahdi Mohammed Ahmed, Nubia became a military territory and was therefore off limits. The war culminated in the fall of Khartoum, which the British army, commanded by General Charles Gordon, had heroically defended. Nevertheless, in 1889 Maspero worked to resume contact with that part of Nubia still under Egyptian control.

David Roberts R.A.   L. Hague lith.

Grand Portico of the Temple of Philæ — Nubia

However, a new danger threatened the Nubian temples: the first dam at Aswan, built between 1898 and 1902, had raised the water level of the Nile, compromising the ancient site in the extreme south. Then, in 1904, the government informed Maspero of its project to raise the height of the dam, to the point that the water-collecting reservoir would have reached Wadi es-Sebua. In winter 1904-1905, Maspero personally visited Lower Nubia and in the following year invited Arthur Weigall, the inspector of antiquities, to check the whole zone as far as al-Maharraqa. Weigall's report showed that an important group of temples, fortresses, and cities would soon be underwater. Moreover, Abu Simbel, like Amada and Al-Derr, were covered by sand, while the temple of Kalabsha had almost completely collapsed. A few years later, in response to an appeal made by Maspero, a number of young scholars from Germany, France, and Britain arrived in Egypt and, in return for modest compensation, dedicated themselves to the execution and publication of surveys of the Nubian temples. In this way, Gunther Roeder worked at Dabod, Beit al-Wali, and al-Dakka and Henri Gauthier took care of Wadi es-Sebua and Amada, while Aylward Blackman dedicated himself to the temples of a-Maharraqa and al-Derr. The fruit of their labor was the publication of a series of volumes of fundamental importance on the temples of Lower Nubia.

THE EXPLORATION OF NUBIA

47

46-47 Construction of the first Aswan Dam lasted from 1898 to 1902.

47 top The first Aswan Dam proved itself to be very useful, and it was planned to raise it in successive stages.

47 center Thanks to the construction of the dam near the First Cataract, the principle of perennial irrigation could become widespread.

47 bottom The erection of the dam permitted the year-round cultivation of the land and an increased number of annual harvests.

THE EXPLORATION OF NUBIA

48 TOP LEFT IN THIS IMAGE FROM 1850, THE COLOSSI OF RAMSES II ARE STILL COVERED BY THE DESERT SANDS.

48 TOP RIGHT AND 49 TOURISTS FROM THE SECOND HALF OF THE NINETEENTH CENTURY CLIMBING THE COLOSSI AT ABU SIMBEL.

48 BOTTOM AN EGYPTOLOGIST STUDIES ONE OF THE NUMEROUS PLAQUES FOUND IN THE AREA OF THE GREAT TEMPLE OF ABU SIMBEL.

A new event was about to modify decisively the topograsphy of Nubia and the destiny of its monuments. In 1959, the construction of the Aswan High Dam was announced, a project designed to make possible the irrigation of almost two million acres of previously uncultivable land, increasing the Sudan's productive area by about 25 percent. Contrary to the previous dam, which left the monuments visible for part of the year, this new barrage would have formed an artificial lake of about 310 miles in length, submerging forever the remains of Nubia's ancient past as far south as the Second Cataract.

The news of the construction of the dam raised great concern among scholars. The Nubian temples were part of the world's artistic patrimony, and therefore many people voiced their wish that the monuments be saved. Work on the dam was scheduled to begin in January 1960 and it was thus necessary to act without delay. Thanks to Christiane Desroches-Noblecourt, conservator of the National French Museums at the Louvre, and Sarwat Okasha, the Egyptian cultural minister, UNESCO became involved in order to resolve the problem. On January 9, 1960 construction work on the dam began. Just three months later the Italian Vittorio Veronese, then director general of UNESCO, made an appeal to the world and promoted an initiative to raise the necessary funds for the organization of a rescue campaign for the monuments of Nubia. Thanks to more than 50 nations that responded to the appeal, it was possible to collect a considerable sum and begin work as soon as possible.

In 1960, the temples of Dabod and Qertassi were dismantled to be rebuilt in a safer location; two years later, the temples of al-Dakka, Dendur, and al-Maharraqa were saved; soon thereafter, that of Kalabsha was dismantled and later reassembled; in 1963, the temples of Qertassi and Buhen; and then in the next year, the temples of Beit al-Wali, Wadi es-Sebua; Amada, Gerf Hussein, and the tomb of Pennut at Aniba were saved.

THE TEMPLES

50 bottom Every single block of Abu Simbel was put in a sling and lifted by crane.

50-51 The photograph shows the two temples of Abu Simbel before their dismantling began.

51 bottom right The interior of the great temple began to be dismantled because of work on the Aswan Dam.

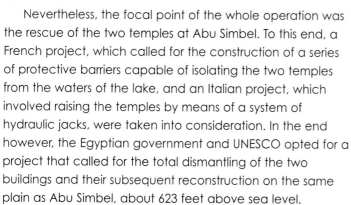

Nevertheless, the focal point of the whole operation was the rescue of the two temples at Abu Simbel. To this end, a French project, which called for the construction of a series of protective barriers capable of isolating the two temples from the waters of the lake, and an Italian project, which involved raising the temples by means of a system of hydraulic jacks, were taken into consideration. In the end however, the Egyptian government and UNESCO opted for a project that called for the total dismantling of the two buildings and their subsequent reconstruction on the same plain as Abu Simbel, about 623 feet above sea level.

The contract was entrusted to a corporation (Abu Simbel Joint Venture), which united companies from various nations: Egypt, France, Germany, Italy, and Sweden. Project coordination was entrusted to a company from Essen, Germany, which had already participated in the dismantling and reconstruction of the temple of Kalabsha.

In April 1964, the construction of a provisionary barrier between the temples and the Nile was started that would hold back the water that had already begun to rise. Early on, the stelae engraved on the hills around the temples were detached from the rock and the statues were removed from the balustrade. Before starting to separate the stone blocks, the two temple façades were covered with a layer of sand in order to protect them; a sheet-metal conduit cut through the accumulation of sand and allowed those who worked inside to enter and exit the temple easily. Finally, the dismantling work began. The separation process was carried out using motorized saws or, in the most difficult cases, handsaws. Every sandstone block of the temple was then reinforced by injections of artificial resin. Every single block was then numbered, lifted, and wrapped in a protective jute canvas, and placed on a truck to be transported to a storage area where it waited to be reassembled. On March 5, 1965, the last block of the small temple was brought to the warehouse, whereas on March 29 the last block of the great temple was removed. All together, 1,035 blocks, weighing between 22 and 33 tons, were detached.

The sanctuaries of Abu Simbel were later rebuilt on the plain that overlooks the site where they once stood, maintaining their original orientation and placement.

52 TOP LEFT THE TERM 'COLOSSUS' IS RIGHTFULLY APPLIED TO THE STATUES OF ABU SIMBEL.

52 TOP RIGHT THIS PHASE OF THE DISMANTLEMENT, INCLUDING MOVING THE FOUR STATUES, TOOK PLACE BETWEEN 1965 AND 1966.

52 BOTTOM THE COLOSSUS' ENORMOUS URAEUS STICKS OUT FROM THE SCAFFOLDING SURROUNDING ONE OF THE HEADS OF THE STATUES OF THE KING.

53 THE HEAD OF ONE OF THE COLOSSI OF RAMESSES II, AFTER HAVING HAD ITS DOUBLE CROWN REMOVED, WAS LIFTED AND MOVED.

On January 26, 1966, reassembly of the first blocks of the great temple began, and in March of the same year, rebuilding of the small temple started. All the blocks, each one marked with a seal indicating its level and position, were reassembled in the exact position they had occupied in the original construction. The reconstruction work ended on September 9, 1967 with the placement of the last block of the façade of the big temple.

In order to recreate the temples' original environment and setting, construction of two artificial hills was planned, given that the two monuments were originally cut out of the rock. To avoid the two temples being crushed by the filling material that crowned the two artificial hills, they were protected by two domes of reinforced cement, on which were thrown tons of rocky debris. Even the stone stelae, the terrace statues, and the temples' adjoining chapels returned to their place. Finally, the technicians studied a way to ensure rewarding visits to the two temples by installing ventilation and artificial lighting systems, both inside and out.

The entire job of dismantling and reconstruction was concluded some fourteen days earlier than anticipated in the contract with Abu Simbel Joint Venture.

A final task remained, one that fell within the professional knowledge of the archeologists. The junction lines in the façades that corresponded to the cutting process were eliminated using a sand paste of a similar color to that of the

surrounding stone blocks; the junction lines of the decorated surfaces in the internal rooms were also erased. As an incidental note on contemporary concerns, it should be added that a copy of the Quran, some Egyptian coins of the time, two Cairo newspapers, and a commemorative document were placed under two blocks standing in the new location.

At last, on September 22, 1968, a magnificent ceremony was held to inaugurate the two temples of Abu Simbel that, in accordance with Ramesses II's wishes, seemed destined to stand forever.

54-55 THE STEEL FRAMEWORK OF THE BIG ARCH THAT WOULD SUPPORT THE WEIGHT OF THE ARTIFICIAL HILLS FRAMING THE STATUES RISES BEHIND THE COLOSSI.

55 JUST LIKE THE GREAT TEMPLE, THE SMALL TEMPLE WAS ALSO TAKEN APART BLOCK BY BLOCK AND FAITHFULLY RECONSTRUCTED.

56-57 *MOVING THE TEMPLES OF ABU SIMBEL WAS THE RESULT OF INTERNATIONAL COOPERATION. EGYPT WAS THUS ABLE TO BENEFIT FROM THE ADVANTAGES CREATED BY THE NEW DAM'S CONSTRUCTION WITHOUT HAVING TO SACRIFICE A PART OF ITS ARCHAEOLOGICAL HERITAGE.*

56 *BOTTOM THE FOUR COLOSSI OF RAMESSES II WERE REASSEMBLED WITH A LARGE SUPPORTING TRESTLE AT THEIR BACK.*

THE RESCUE OF
THE TEMPLES

*57 BOTTOM LEFT THE PHOTO
DOCUMENTS A PHASE IN THE
RECONSTRUCTION WORK OF THE
SMALL TEMPLE OF ABU SIMBEL.*

*57 RIGHT A WORKER INJECTS A
RESINOUS SUBSTANCE INTO THE
HEAD OF A COLOSSUS TO ENSURE
THAT THE STONE DOES NOT
CRUMBLE DURING THE
CONSTRUCTION PROCESS.*

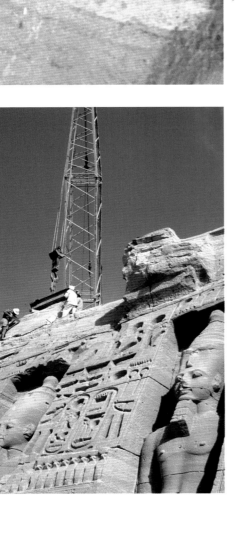

As said before, the Nubian monuments threatened by the construction of the Great Aswan Dam were many. The fate of the sanctuary of Isis on Philae Island was similar to that of Abu Simbel. Thanks to a UNESCO campaign, over nine million dollars, donated by several countries, were raised for the rescue of the monuments on the site. The Italian company Condotte-Mazzi Abroad won the international competition for the contract, announced in 1969, to perform topographical and architectural surveys and then dismantle the 45,000 blocks of the buildings. Using the photogrammetric technique, they were then able to rebuild the structures in their exact original form on nearby Agilkia Island, close to Philae but 'higher' by 43 feet. While the dismantling procedure took place, concluding on November 30, 1976, little more than a year after the actual start of construction, Agilkia Island was being prepared to accommodate the monuments. The perimeter of the island was modified and even its plant life was made similar to that of Philae. When construction finished, in 1977 Philae Island submerged under the water, while the reconstructed temple was finally inaugurated in its new and final location on March 10, 1980.

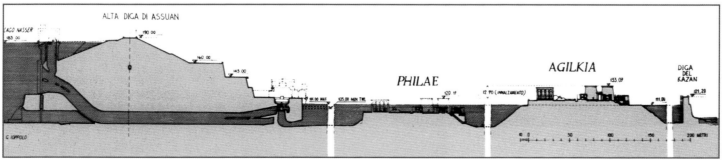

58 TOP EACH BLOCK OF THE
TEMPLE OF PHILAE, REMOVED BY
HAND WITH A LEVER, WAS
SECURED INTO A SLING WITH
STEEL BRACES LINED IN NYLON.

58 CENTER THE PHOTOGRAPH
SHOWS PHILAE ISLAND DURING

THE DISMANTLING OF ITS
MONUMENTS.

58 BOTTOM TO AVOID FURTHER
FLOODING, THE MONUMENTS
OF PHILAE WERE REBUILT
ON AGILKIA ISLAND.

58-59 AFTER HAVING BEEN
LIFTED BY CRANES, THE BLOCKS
WERE CARRIED ON A PLATFORM
ALONG THE EAST SIDE OF THE
ISLAND AND LOADED ONTO
BARGES TO THEN BE MOVED TO
THE STORAGE AREA.

59 TOP THE BLOCKS' STORAGE
AREA WAS WELL ORGANIZED: EACH
MONUMENT WAS SEPARATED INTO
ITS OWN ROW OF SANDSTONE
BLOCKS, AND THE LANES OF THE
DEPOSIT WERE NAMED AFTER THE
MONUMENT HELD THERE.

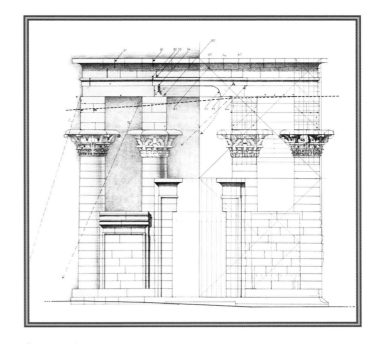

60-61 THE FIRST PYLON OF THE TEMPLE OF ISIS SURROUNDED BY SCAFFOLDING.

61 TOP MEASUREMENTS TAKEN FOR THE BUILDING'S DISMANTLEMENT CAN BE SEEN ON THIS DRAWING OF THE KIOSK OF TRAJAN.

61 CENTER AND BOTTOM BEFORE STARTING TO MOVE THE MONUMENTS, IT WAS NECESSARY TO DRAIN PHILAE ISLAND, WHICH WAS FLOODED BY THE NILE FOR SIX MONTHS A YEAR.

THE GREAT TEMPLE

T he great temple at Abu Simbel is certainly one of the most famous places of worship in all of Egypt. Built on the western bank of the Nile by Pharaoh Ramesses II, the building was simply called "the temple of Ramesses-Meryamun" (Ramses-beloved of Amun) by the ancient Egyptians.

From the river, by means of a stone pier, visitors arrive at the gate that gives access to the front courtyard from which, by a nine-step staircase divided in two by a narrow ramp, a terrace is reached. Here, visitors find themselves facing the façade of

AT ABU SIMBEL

the temple, entirely excavated from the rock. Ramesses' architect, having had to forgo the pylons typical of Egyptian temples, transformed the rock wall of the mountain into a terraced podium. From this rose four colossal statues of the seated pharaoh, each about 69 feet tall and leaning against a structure that simulates the façade of a pylon, 105 feet tall and 125 feet wide at the base. The four statues portray the sovereign with the short kilt, the typical pharaonic fabric head-covering called a *nemes*, the double crown with the uraeus on the front, and the stylized false beard.

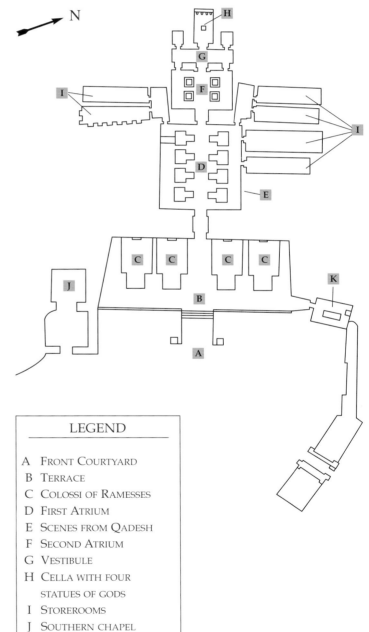

N

LEGEND

A   FRONT COURTYARD
B   TERRACE
C   COLOSSI OF RAMESSES
D   FIRST ATRIUM
E   SCENES FROM QADESH
F   SECOND ATRIUM
G   VESTIBULE
H   CELLA WITH FOUR
    STATUES OF GODS
I   STOREROOMS
J   SOUTHERN CHAPEL
K   SOLAR ALTAR

66 TOP THE SCENE ILLUSTRATED
UNDER THE KING'S CARTOUCHE
SYMBOLIZES THE UNIFICATION OF
EGYPT. THE PERSONIFICATIONS
OF THE NORTHERN AND
SOUTHERN NILE TIE BETWEEN
THEM THE EMBLEMATIC PLANTS
OF UPPER AND LOWER EGYPT.

66-67 ON THE BASE OF ONE OF
THE COLOSSI, SYMBOLICALLY
PLACED UNDER THE KING'S FEET,
NUBIAN PRISONERS ARE
PORTRAYED CHAINED AND
WEARING THEIR TRADITIONAL
DRESS, A SHORT KILT HELD UP BY
A BALDRIC AND A SCARF THAT
FALLS ACROSS THE CHEST.

67 TOP LEFT THE NICHE ABOVE
THE DOOR, FLANKED BY TWO
ILLUSTRATIONS OF RAMESSES II
AT WORSHIP, CONTAINS A STATUE
OF RA, A PICTURE OF MAAT,
AND AN USER SCEPTER, WHICH
ALL TOGETHER FORM THE FIRST
NAME OF THE KING.

67 RIGHT IN THIS STATUE, RAMESSES IS PORTRAYED WITH THE ATTRIBUTES OF OSIRIS, A DOUBLE CROWN, A CLOTH HEAD COVERING, AND TWO SCEPTERS EMBLEMATIC OF ROYALTY.

68-69 THE FOUR COLOSSI WERE EACH GIVEN THEIR OWN NAMES: THE SOUTHERN ONES WERE CALLED "RAMESSES, SUN OF THE KINGS" AND "SOVEREIGN OF THE TWO LANDS," WHEREAS THE NORTHERN ONES WERE "RAMESSES, BELOVED OF AMUN" AND "BELOVED OF ATUM."

Next to the legs of the four colossi are several smaller standing statues that represent the pharaoh's relatives. These comprise three statues of the 'Great Royal Bride' Nefertari; two of the queen Mut-tuy, wife of Seti I and mother of Ramesses II; one of the princes Amenherkhopshef and Ramesses; and one of the princesses Bint-Anath, Nebettawi, Merytamun, and a nameless fourth one.

Above the temple entrance, a niche with a sculptural group has been carved that represents the praenomen of Ramesses II, User-maat-ra, in cryptographic writing--a sort of riddle. The group includes the statue of Ra, with a human body and the head of a falcon, with the goddess Maat, the Egyptian conception of correct order, at his left leg; while by the side of his right leg is a hieroglyph that depicts the stylized head and neck of an animal and reads user (meaning 'powerful'). At the top of the temple façade, there is a row of 22 squatting

baboon statues. The baboon's cry was believed to welcome the rising sun. The distance from the border of the podium to the cella (the spiritually important inner chamber) in the back of the temple, oriented exactly east, measures 207 feet. As in other temples with inner chambers, in this temple, the floor inclines slightly, the ceiling lowers, and the walls tighten progressively as the visitor nears the cella in the rear, the sanctum sanctorum, which holds the sacred boat of the gods.

70 On the ceiling of the first atrium, illustrations of crowned vultures with spread wings can be seen gripping two feather fans in their claws to protect the cartouches of the sovereign.

70-71 The Osirian pillars on the right wear the double crown, whereas those on the left wear the white crown of Upper Egypt.

Once past the threshold of the big temple's entrance, visitors enter a room (the first atrium) divided into a nave and two aisles with eight 33-foot pillars that depict the pharaoh in the likeness of the god Osiris. The central nave is double the width of the side aisles, and the Osirid pillars are linteled. From this room, through a doorway, which originally must have had double doors, the second atrium is entered. It is smaller, with a central nave and two aisles divided by four pillars featuring scenes on each façade in which the king is received and embraced by the gods. Continuing toward the rear of the temple, visitors arrive at a vestibule that extends along the axis and, at the end, with two side cellae, is the central *sanctum sanctorum*. This features on the back wall, in life size, the statues of the gods Ptah of Memphis, Amon-Ra of Thebes, a deified Ramesses II, and Ra-Harakhty of Heliopolis, sitting on a low bench carved, like the statues, out of the rock.

From the first atrium, through two lateral openings, two groups of storerooms are reached, arranged like horizontal "combs" relative to the main axis of the temple: these eight spaces were intended for the deposit of objects and furnishings for worship ceremonies in the temple.

Unfortunately, the original lively colors that embellished the reliefs of the sanctuary have been lost.

THE GREAT TEMPLE

72 TOP RAMESSES II OFFERS A
TRAY OVERFLOWING WITH FOOD
TO THE GOD HORUS OF BAKI.

72-73 ON THE PILLARS OF THE
SECOND ATRIUM, RAMESSES II IS
PORTRAYED EMBRACING VARIOUS
DIVINITIES AS A SIGN OF HIS
SPIRITUAL UNION AND
PREDILECTION.

73 TOP THE SECOND ATRIUM,
WHOSE WALLS FEATURE SCENES
AND INSCRIPTIONS OF A RELIGIOUS
NATURE, IS ACCESSED THROUGH
THE FIRST ATRIUM.

73 BOTTOM FROM THE SECOND
ATRIUM, ONE PASSES INTO THE
VESTIBULE. IN THE FOREGROUND,
THE PHARAOH IS PORTRAYED
MAKING OFFERINGS.

In the first atrium, on the north wall, there is an immense relief that records the battle of Qadesh in Syria against the Hittites. On the south wall, there are other military-themed reliefs whose colors have been partially preserved: for example, a few scenes showing hostilities against Libya and Nubia, Ramesses II in his war chariot with his bow, and the siege of an enemy city.

On the lateral walls of the second atrium, scenes have been preserved that show the procession of the sacred boat, while others depict the pharaoh holding out offerings to various gods. It must be noted that the artistic technique and accuracy of the reliefs gradually diminish along the way

toward the interior of the building. The relief depicting the Battle of Qadesh, 30 feet tall and 56 wide, is drawn with great care, full of figures, details, and vivacity, but the scenes in the second atrium were executed in a less accurate manner, often finished with painted stucco-work. The reliefs of the *sanctum sanctorum* were perhaps even more perfunctory and less precise. The artists that offered their services in the temple might have felt gradually weighed down by fatigue and the great quantity of labor as they neared the conclusion of the temple's decoration.

Outside the temple, next to the southern extremity of the façade, stands a small stone chapel, opposite a brick atrium, dedicated by Ramesses II to the gods Amun and Ra. On the other hand, at the northern extremity, is a small stone solar altar placed between two obelisks, one of which associates the pharaoh with Ra-Harakhty and the other with Atum, both divinities of a solar nature.

74 RAMESSES II, PROTECTED BY THE VULTURE GODDESS NEKHBET, MASSACRES HIS ENEMIES.

74-75 ON THE NORTH WALL OF THE FIRST ATRIUM, RAMESSES II IS PORTRAYED ON THE THRONE BEFORE THE BATTLE OF QADESH.

76-77 RAMESSES II, FIRING ARROWS, STORMS INTO THE RANKS OF HIS ENEMIES WITH HIS CHARIOT.

77 THE CITY OF QADESH WAS BORDERED BY TWO RIVERS AND A CANAL.

78 *The ranks of the Egyptian army were the main instrument in the campaign against the Hittities, which concluded in the battle of Qadesh on the Orontes River.*

79 TOP *The uniform and head covering distinguish these characters as two foreign soldiers.*

79 TOP CENTER *Thanks to these reliefs, the battle of Qadesh is the earliest in history whose various phases can be observed.*

79 BOTTOM CENTER *Two Hittite explorers captured by the Egyptians are forced to reveal the enemy's position. The text recounts that they gave false information to lead the Egyptian army into a trap; nonetheless, Ramesses II managed to get the better of his enemy, thanks to the help of Amon.*

79 BOTTOM *The Egyptian soldiers armed with shields are accompanied by a trumpet player.*

80 TOP
During the New Kingdom, the King was accompanied to war by a domesticated lion.

80 BOTTOM AND *81* *Like the horse, the chariot was*

introduced into Egypt by the Hyksos around 1600 B.C.

82-83 *Ramesses kills a Libyan with a lance. The scene has been copied from a relief in the temple of Karnak.*

THE GREAT TEMPLE

84-85 From the second atrium, whose walls still bear some of the original colorings, the rear cella can be glimpsed with its cult statues.

85 top The vulture represents the goddess Nekhbet, the protective divinity of Upper Egypt.

85 bottom Ramesses II is flanked, in this statuary group, by the three main dynastic gods of the New Kingdom, Ptah, Amun-Ra, and Ra-Harakhty. This iconography raises him to the level of divinity.

86-87 Ramesses II, followed by Queen Nefertari shaking two sistrums, burns incense in front of the sacred boat of Amun-Ra. A statue of the divinity led in procession by priests was located inside the tabernacle on the boat. Its bow and stern are adorned by ram heads with the solar disk that represented the god Amun.

THE SMALL TEMPLE

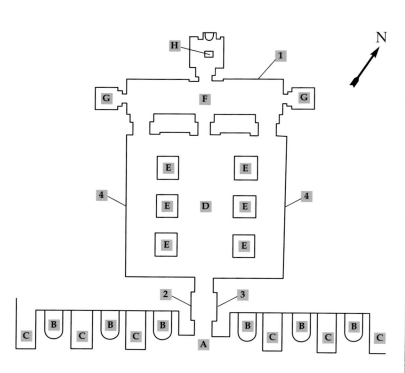

The small temple at Abu Simbel, situated not far from the great temple, was dedicated by Ramesses II to the goddess Hathor of Ibshek, a small village not far from Abu Simbel, and to his 'Great Royal Bride.' It was not the first time that a temple was dedicated to a queen in Egypt; however here, for the first time, some statues of a queen, as tall as those of the king, appear on the façade of a temple. On each side of the façade's entrance are three niches in which were carved, directly out of the rock, six 33-foot-tall statues, four portraying the pharaoh and two the queen. The king wears the characteristic short kilt; he is portrayed wearing various crowns; the double crown symbolizing the union of Upper and Lower Egypt, the white crown of Upper Egypt, or a head covering composed of a ram's horn surmounted by a solar disc with two tall ostrich feathers. Queen Nefertari is depicted with a solar disc with two tall feathers between the horns of the cow-goddess Hathor on her head. The rulers are portrayed standing, with their left legs slightly forward, as if the sculptures were about to free themselves from the temple façade. Each of the statues has a reduced-scale statue of the royal couple's children by their side: the princes Ra-her-unemef, Amenherkhepsnef, Meryatum, and Meryra, and the princesses Henuttawi, and Merytamun; oddly, the statues of the princesses are taller than those of the princes (perhaps because the temple pays tribute to femininity?). In addition, buttresses covered with deeply carved hieroglyphic inscriptions separate the large statues from each other.

88-89 THE TWO TEMPLES OF ABU SIMBEL ARE THE APOGEE OF ROCK ARCHITECTURE IN NUBIA.

AT ABU SIMBEL

89 TOP THE TWO CARTOUCHES, FOUND ABOVE THE TEMPLE'S ENTRANCE, CONTAIN THE NAME AND GIVEN NAME OF RAMESSES II.

90-91 THE COLOSSI IN THE NICHES OF THE SMALL TEMPLE PORTRAY NEFERTARI AND HER SPOUSE RAMESSES II.

The small temple's layout is simpler than that of the great temple. Beyond the threshold, overlooked by a frieze of uraeuses, an entrance opens onto a hall with a central nave and two aisles divided by two rows of three Hathoric pillars (pillars that reproduce the face of the goddess Hathor). On the back wall of the room, corresponding to the nave and aisles, there are three openings that lead to a vestibule positioned across the axis and whose reliefs show Nefertari in the act of being crowned by the goddesses Hathor and Isis. She is wearing a head covering identical to that which the goddesses themselves are wearing: the solar disc with feathers between cow horns. At the sides of the vestibule, two small, undecorated rooms open while a central door gives access to the *sanctum sanctorum*, on whose back walls, slightly to the right, a niche is found with a portrayal of the goddess Hathor in the likeness of a cow.

The scenes present on the walls of the small temple are for the most part of a religious nature. On the left of the internal part of the entrance, the king is depicted paying homage to Hathor, and on the right, Nefertari is depicted in the act of adoration of Isis. In the atrium, there are some scenes in which Ramesses II, in the company of Nefertari, carries out the ritual killing of a Libyan enemy before Ra and also a Nubian enemy in front of Amun. There are also some scenes in which the pharaoh pays homage to various divinities of the Egyptian pantheon.

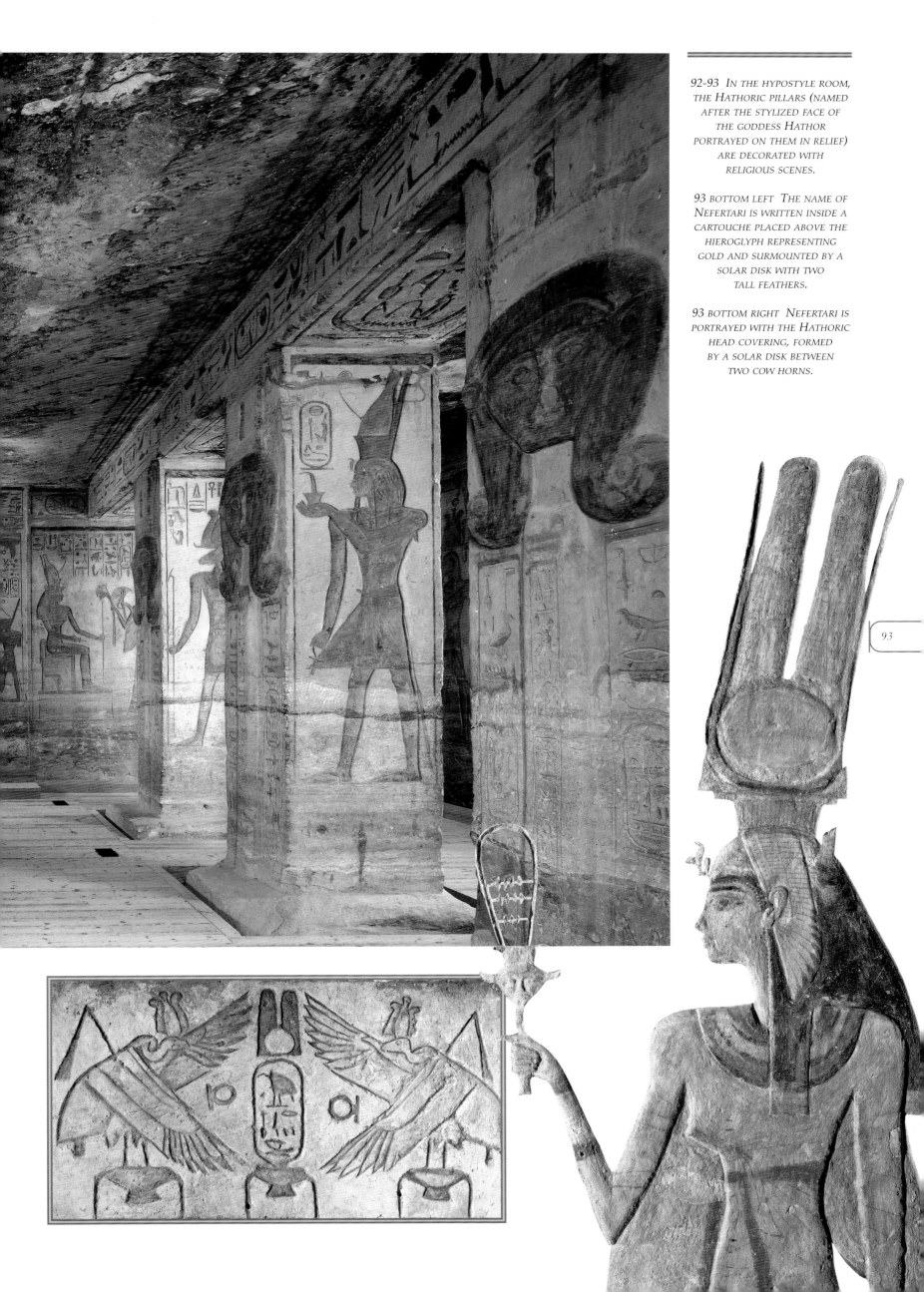

92-93 IN THE HYPOSTYLE ROOM, THE HATHORIC PILLARS (NAMED AFTER THE STYLIZED FACE OF THE GODDESS HATHOR PORTRAYED ON THEM IN RELIEF) ARE DECORATED WITH RELIGIOUS SCENES.

93 BOTTOM LEFT THE NAME OF NEFERTARI IS WRITTEN INSIDE A CARTOUCHE PLACED ABOVE THE HIEROGLYPH REPRESENTING GOLD AND SURMOUNTED BY A SOLAR DISK WITH TWO TALL FEATHERS.

93 BOTTOM RIGHT NEFERTARI IS PORTRAYED WITH THE HATHORIC HEAD COVERING, FORMED BY A SOLAR DISK BETWEEN TWO COW HORNS.

It is not known for certain when construction of the temples at Abu Simbel began. However, it is certain that the great temple's decoration was begun before Ramesses II's 26th regnal year since Prince Ramesses, third-born of the king, died before that year, while in the temple he is portrayed three times without the typical epithets that the ancient Egyptians attached to the deceased. The decoration of the main rooms of the big temple was likewise finished by the pharaoh's 34th regnal year: because there was no room inside the temple, the so-called 'marriage stela' depicting Ramesses II's union with a Hittite princess was placed outside, on the rock wall that delimits the façade on the south side. Most likely, Nefertari died before the decoration of the big temple was finished. The king's daughter Bint-Anath, who appears with the simple title of princess on the statue placed at the leg of one of the colossi outside, was instead portrayed as the "Great Royal Bride" in the lower registers of the first atrium's reliefs. Therefore, the construction of the great temple was essentially finished and its decoration begun before the death of Prince Ramesses (in his father's 26th regnal year). The decoration of the building had to be finished toward the 34th regnal year. At that time, Ramesses II had already lost his two 'Great Royal Brides,' Nefertari and Isis-neferet, and had married his first-born daughter born of Isis-neferet, Bint-Anath, who was still

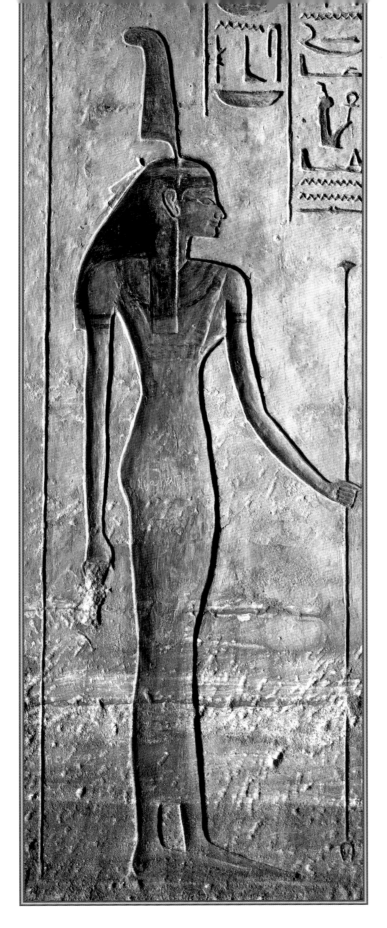

alive in his 44th regnal year, when another Nubian temple was built at Wadi es-Sebua, where she again appears as queen.

Unfortunately, it is not known when the temple was completely abandoned and began to become covered by sand. However, it is known that the build-up was already in quite an advanced state when the troops of Psammetichus II (Twenty-sixth Dynasty) led a military campaign in Nubia in 591 B.C. Between the 6th and the 2nd centuries B.C., the entrance to the temple would have been barely accessible. Then, over time, the sand covered nearly all of the building. In the 7th century A.D., only the head and shoulders of colossus at the far left of the entrance, the incomplete torso of the one nearest the temple's entrance, and the crowns of the two colossi at the right remained above the sand. The monument remained hidden in this way until its 'rediscovery' in the nineteenth century.

THE THEOLOGICAL

Every temple in Egypt satisfied particular theological and religious principles. These depended on a variety of factors, first of all the divinities worshipped in the sanctuary, but also the place and period of the temple's construction, possible theological 'ties' with other nearby sanctuaries, and so on. The temples at Abu Simbel are not an exception. With their construction, Ramesses II did not simply aim to emphasize the influence Egypt wielded over Nubia, from which it obtained gold, metal, livestock, and exotic products. As it will be seen, in the great temple the pharaoh intended to carry out a complex plan of theological speculation on his own deification while he was still alive, while in the small temple, he tried to identify his beloved Queen Nefertari with the goddess Hathor of Ibshek.

The four colossal statues of the big temple's façade have a strong psychological impact since they take the exaltation of the figure of the pharaoh to an extreme level. However, Ramesses II did nothing other than to proceed with a plan prepared in advance by his predecessors of the Eighteenth Dynasty, who intended to raise their human qualities to the

maximum level. These included, for example, the courage of Thutmosis III, the physical strength of Amenhotep II, and in the case of Amenhotep III, the exaltation of the figure of the pharaoh. He, long before Ramesses II reigned, had had a temple built at Soleb, in Upper Nubia, in which he venerated his own living image on earth.

The deification of the living Ramesses II in the great temple and the linking of Queen Nefertari to the divine world in the small temple was possible thanks to theological support offered by two Nubian divinities. These were Horus of Meha (the Egyptian name of the place where the Abu Simbel temples were built) and Hathor of Ibshek, a small village that may have been situated to the north of Meha.

The introduction of the cult of the god Horus in Nubia probably dates back to the Middle Kingdom. In order to

facilitate the assimilation of Lower Nubia into Egypt, Pharaoh Senusret III (Twelfth Dynasty) consecrated four sites to the Egyptian god: Baki (Quban), Mi'am (Aniba), Buhen (now Wadi Halfa, just south the Second Cataract), and Meha. The presence of Horus made it possible for his usual consort also to be present, the goddess Hathor, venerated at Abu Simbel in the local form of Hathor of Ibshek.

The reliefs in the big temple show how Ramesses II decided early on to identify himself with Horus of Meha. On the first pillar of the southern row in the room with the Osirid pillars, Nefertari is seen standing before Hathor of Ibshek. Above this scene, the pharaoh is seen making offerings to a falcon-headed divinity with a human ear and a ram's horn. This god is called by Ramesses II's complete praenomen, User-maat-ra setep-en-ra, when one would actually expect, above the figure of Hathor of Ibshek, to see that of her husband, Horus of Meha. Moreover, this scene is already an early example of how Ramesses II could be portrayed giving offerings to himself. In one of the side chambers off the Osirid-pillared room, there are, on the western wall, scenes oriented south to north and dedicated to the gods Amun-Ra of Thebes, Ra-Harakhty of Heliopolis, Ramses-meryamun (Ramesses II's name) and, portrayed as a falcon-headed god and called "great god,"are Horus of Buhen, Horus of Mi'am, and Horus of Baki. It is obvious that even in this context that Ramesses II occupied the place of Horus of Meha, who is missing here.

CONCEPT OF ABU SIMBEL

THE GREAT TEMPLE

The deification of Ramesses II happened, in all probability, in successive steps.

At the beginning, it was applied, through identification of the local version of Horus of Meha with one of the embodiments of the king, specifically with the one that is expressed by his praenomen, User-maat-ra, the name taken by Ramesses II at the time of his coronation. Perhaps at a later date, his deification was extended to the entire person of the pharaoh. The divinity, as a matter of fact, is no longer designated by the praenomen, but by the name Ramses-meryamun, the name that Ramesses II was given at birth. In addition, the fact that Ramesses II is called "great god," an epithet often attributed to the most important Egyptian divinities, implies that the pharaoh, in his lifetime, had to all effects already acquired the privileges of a god. At this point, it should not be surprising that years after construction of the big temple at Abu Simbel was complete, in another Nubian temple, that of Wadi es-Sebua, Ramesses II substituted himself yet again as a god in place of Horus of Meha.

In the pillared hall of this temple, the king is actually portrayed making offerings to Ptah, to himself, and to Hathor, and then the other three Nubian Horuses (those of Baki, Mi'am, and Buhen) and the primordial god Atum.

Toward the rear of the great temple at Abu Simbel, further proof is encountered of the pharaoh's deification and how it developed over time. On the lateral walls of the hypostyle hall, which comes after the hall with with the Osirid pillars, there are scenes depicting the procession of the sacred boat. Queen Nefertari can be seen in the act of shaking a sistrum (a rattle of the tambourine type), while the pharaoh, with a scepter in hand, spreads incense before the path of the boat of Amun. On the northern wall, Ramesses II is portrayed making offerings to the gods Min of Coptos, Horus of Meha, the ram god Khnum of Elephantine, Atum of Heliopolis, Thoth of Hermopolis, and Ptah of Memphis. On another wall of the same room, a scene appears in which Ramesses II gives flowers to the Theban god Amun and his consort Mut and to himself as a god.

It must be emphasized that, at an earlier time, Amon and Mut were depicted sitting on a throne in this scene. At a later time, Ramesses II as a god, sitting on a throne with the solar disc on his head, was inserted between the two divinities; the figure of Mut, placed behind that of the king-god, was changed from her previous seated position to a standing one. The modification made to this scene was the result of a new theological phase. Ramesses II was no longer simply identified with the local Horus (Horus of Meha); the king-god had now become part of a triad, or a group of three gods, in this case a genuine divine family. Ramesses II could therefore take the place of Khonsu, the son of Amon and Mut, and elsewhere, still by the same theological principle, substitute the young god Nefertum between his divine parents Ptah and Sekhmet of Memphis.

102 RAMESSES II OFFERS HATHOR WINE, A DRINK PARTICULARLY APPRECIATED BY THE GODDESS, OFTEN ASSOCIATED WITH THE CONCEPTS OF JOY, LOVE, AND DRUNKENNESS.

103 LEFT RAMESSES II GIVES LETTUCE, A VEGETABLE CONSIDERED TO HOLD APHRODISIACAL PROPERTIES, TO THE GOD AMUN, PORTRAYED WITH AN ERECT MEMBER AND FOLLOWED BY THE GODDESS ISIS.

103 TOP RIGHT THE PHARAOH, WITH THE DOUBLE CROWN ON HIS HEAD, OFFERS BREAD TO THE GOD ATUM, PORTRAYED WEARING THE WHITE CROWN OF UPPER EGYPT.

103 BOTTOM RIGHT THE GOD PTAH, PORTRAYED WITH A MUMMIFORM BODY, HAS HIS HEAD COVERED WITH A SMOOTH CAP.

As if this were not enough, in the rear cella, Ramesses II is portrayed spreading incense for the sacred boat and offering fabric to himself as a god, with his head surmounted by the solar disc.

Only the two 'extremities' of the temple remain to be examined: the outer façade and the rear wall of the cella. It was stated earlier that above the temple's entrance, in a niche, User-maat-ra, the praenomen of Ramesses II, was expressed in cryptographic writing. The position of the relief leaves no room for doubt: the great temple at Abu Simbel was built by Ramesses II for Ramesses II.

It was also stated earlier that four sitting statues of gods were carved on the cella's rear wall. The temple was built in such a way that twice a year, as the sun appeared on the horizon, its rays would penetrate the hall with the Osirid pillars, passing through the hypostyle hall, the vestibule, and the cella until they illuminated the four-statue group in the back comprising the pharaoh in the company of the three most important divinities of the Ramesside era. The architects of the temple, who obviously planned the layout of the building before its construction, kept this particular phenomenon in mind and acted in such as way as to take advantage of it for religious purposes. Nevertheless, it is not known if this phenomenon occurred in keeping with particular dates or events in Ramesses II's reign, for example, on his birthday or on the anniversary of his ascent to the throne. It is, however, worth mentioning the fact that the statue of Ramesses II, like that of Ra-Harakhty and Amun, both solar divinities, shone twice a year in the light of the sun inside the temple. On the other hand, the statue of Ptah who, like the Memphite god Soker had ties to the world of the dead, was not fully hit by the rays of the sun, but only on the left shoulder.

THE SMALL TEMPLE

106 THE GODDESS MUT, HERE CALLED THE 'LADY OF THE SKY, RULER OF THE GODS,' RECEIVES FLOWERS FROM NEFERTARI, PORTRAYED WITH A LOOSE DRESS AND THE HATHORIC HEAD COVERING.

107 NEFERTARI MAKES A DONATION OF TWO SISTRUMS TO THE GODDESS HATHOR. THE OFFERING OF THESE MUSICAL INSTRUMENTS HAD THE PURPOSE OF PLACATING THE GODDESS' RAGE.

It could be questioned if the deification of Ramesses II in the great temple implies a similar process for Queen Nefertari in the small temple. However, the uniqueness of this sanctuary is immediately evident; in fact, for the first time, two statues of a queen, as tall as those of the king, appear on the façade of an Egyptian temple. The temple reliefs present the queen in the act of performing rituals before various feminine divinities. For example, inside the pillared hall there are scenes in which Nefertari shakes the sistrum before the goddesses Hathor, Mut, and Anukis. In the scenes on the pillars, the queen takes on the likeness of Isis and Mut. It is interesting how in the small temple the scenes tend to glorify the divine 'maternity.' There are depictions of Mut, whose name means 'mother;' of Tauret, the goddess of childbirth; Anukis breast-feeding the child king; the sacred cow Hathor; and the goddess Isis, bride of Osiris and mother par excellence, having given birth to the god Horus with whom reigning pharaohs were identified. The same identification of Nefertari with Hathor of Ibshek was meant to present the 'Great Royal Bride' of Ramesses II as a mother.

Hathor of Ibshek is actually none other than one of the many aspects of the great Hathor of Dendera, the sacred cow that nursed and protected from birth the young princes destined to ascend the throne of Egypt.

Unfortunately, Nefertari died before work on the big temple was finished and therefore before the complete deification of the pharaoh. As such, it is impossible to know if the "Great Royal Bride" would have been simply identified with Hathor of Ibshek in the small temple or if Ramesses II intended to raise her, in her lifetime, to a divine level.

Lastly, it must be remembered that in the rear cella the base where the sacred processional boat should have been set down—an essential element in Egyptian temples—is missing. The only boat that appears in the small temple is portrayed above one of the doors of the vestibule; on it the goddess Hathor navigates among the papyrus shoots, while Nefertari offers her flowers. This peculiarity of the rear cella suggests that the worship ceremonies in the small temple were different from those that were usually celebrated in Egyptian religious edifices.

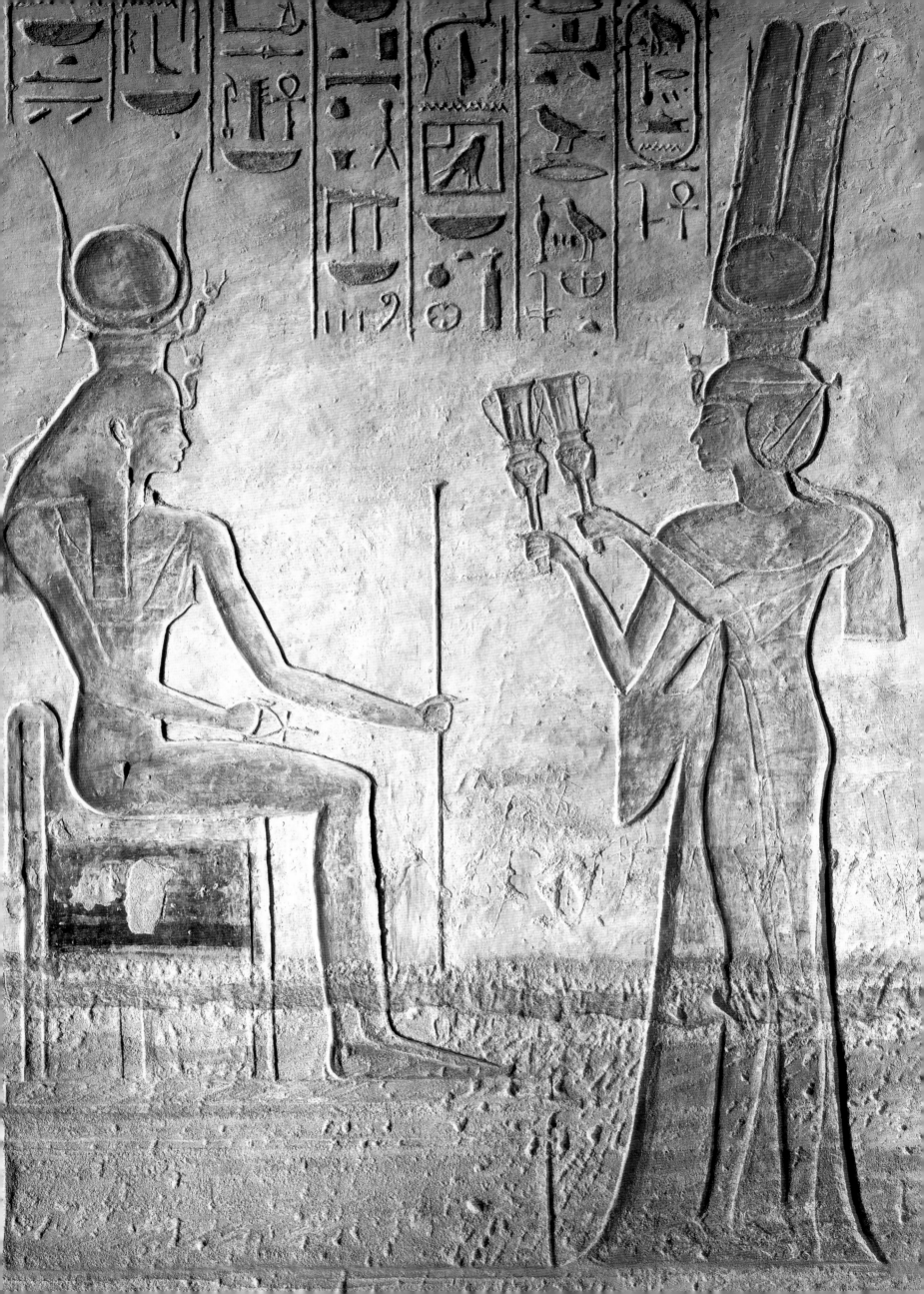

108 TOP NEFERTARI HOLDS OUT
SOME FLOWERS TO THE GODDESS
HATHOR, IN THE ASPECT OF A
COW WITH HER HORNS ADORNED
WITH A SOLAR DISK AND TALL
FEATHERS WHILE FLOATING
ON A BOAT THROUGH
THE PAPYRUS REEDS.

108-109 NEFERTARI, HERE
CALLED THE 'GREAT ROYAL
BRIDE,' OFFERS FLOWERS TO THE
RAM GOD KHNUM AND THE
GODDESSES SATET AND ANUKIS,
WHO CONTROLLED THE
FLOODING OF THE WATERS FROM
ELEPHANTINE ISLAND.

110-111 RAMESSES II IS
PORTRAYED WITH THE BLUE
CROWN AND AN URAEUS ON HIS
FOREHEAD, THE LATTER
A SYMBOL OF ROYALTY,
AS HE GIVES FLOWERS TO
THE GODDESS HATHOR.

SITES AND TEMPLES

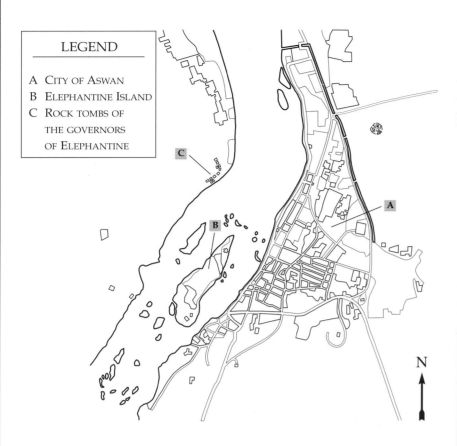

N

ASWAN

Included in the first *nome* (or province) of Upper Egypt, the area around Aswan can be considered the gateway to Nubia and therefore deserves a brief description. The region of the First Cataract was important both for its granite quarries and for commerce with Nubia, in which it had become the leader. Moreover, according to legend, it was here that, hidden among the rocks of the rapids, were the two big caverns from which the River Nile originated.

The modern city of Aswan stands on the eastern bank of the river. Here, the remains of a few temples of the Ptolemaic and Roman eras are found.

112 BOTTOM NEAR ELEPHANTINE ISLAND, THERE ARE SEVERAL SMALL ISLANDS THAT HELP TO CREATE AN EXTREMELY STRIKING PANORAMA.

112-113 ELEPHANTINE ISLAND WAS CONSECRATED TO THE CULT OF THE RAM GOD KHNUM. THE ACTUAL CITY IS FOUND ON THE SOUTHERN SIDE OF THE ISLAND.

113 BOTTOM LEFT SAILING CRAFTS DOT THIS TRACT OF THE NILE RIVER IN THE AREA OF ASWAN.

113 BOTTOM RIGHT THE PHOTOGRAPH SHOWS THE TRACT OF RIVER BETWEEN ASWAN AND ELEPHANTINE ISLAND, WITH SOME RUINS OF THE ANCIENT CITY ON THE LEFT.

IN LOWER NUBIA

West of Aswan, in Nile, is Elephantine Island (the ancient Egyptian Abu), the county seat of the first *nome* of Upper Egypt and the center of the cult of the ram god Khnum and the goddess Satet, the controllers of the Nile's waters. At Elephantine, the remains of the ancient city, already inhabited by the Old Kingdom era, are preserved; there are some remains of temples built by Thutmosis II (Eighteenth Dynasty), Ramesses III (Twentieth Dynasty), and Nectanebo II (Thirtieth Dynasty) and a 'Nilometer,' which served to measure the level of the river.

On the Nile's western bank, on the side of a hill facing the river, the tombs of the governors of Elephantine during the Old and Middle Kingdoms were excavated. These officials, in the name of the pharaoh, governed Nubia.

Continuing south from Aswan, the visitor encounters the granite quarries, already being exploited in ancient times. Opposite them is Sehel Island, where the goddess Anukis, Lady of the Cataracts, resided and where an Eighteenth-Dynasty temple and one from the Ptolemaic era stand.

114 TOP THE TEMPLE OF THE GODDESS SATET HAS RECENTLY BEEN THE OBJECT OF RESTORATION PROJECTS.

114-115 THE CITY OF ASWAN COMPOSES THE BACKGROUND TO THE MODEST DWELLINGS OF A VILLAGE ON ELEPHANTINE ISLAND.

115 TOP LEFT THE ANCIENT CITY
OF ELEPHANTINE WAS FOUNDED
DURING THE EARLIEST
DYNASTIES.

115 TOP RIGHT THIS PILLAR
FEATURING THE FACE OF THE
GODDESS HATHOR IS FOUND IN
THE TEMPLE OF SATET.

116 top left After having been sculpted on three sides, this more than 135-foot-tall granite obelisk was left at the quarry, more likely because of its size than the crack visible on its point.

116 top right In this graffito of Sehel, a man called Imen-em-opet lifts his arms in adoration of the goddess Anukis.

116-117 The name of Elephantine, of Greek origin, is a translation of the ancient Egyptian term Abu, the 'city of the elephant.'

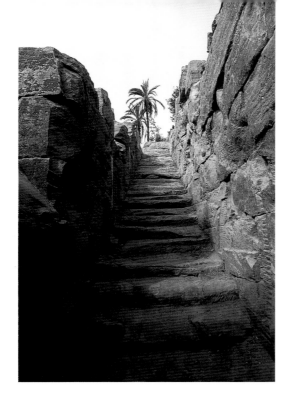

ASWAN

117 TOP LEFT THE NILOMETER (OR HYDROMETER) ON ELEPHANTINE IS FORMED BY A STAIRCASE WITH TWO PERPENDICULAR FLIGHTS FLANKED BY GRADUATED SLABS, WHICH DESCENDS INTO THE RIVER.

117 TOP RIGHT THE MAUSOLEUM OF AGA KHAN STANDS NOT FAR FROM ASWAN.

117 BOTTOM ON THIS ROCK, THE NAMES OF PSAMMETICHUS II, KING OF THE TWENTY-SIXTH DYNASTY, ARE INSCRIBED.

118 TOP AND CENTER *THE CORRIDOR IN THE TOMB OF SARENPUT II LEADS TO THE REAR CELLA WHERE THERE IS A NICHE FOR HIS VENERATION. HE IS PORTRAYED SEATED BEFORE A WELL-LAID TABLE AND HIS SON WHO MAKES OFFERINGS.*

118 BOTTOM *THE ENTRANCE TO THE TOMB OF SARENPUT II IS CUT IN THE SIDE OF THE HILL OVERLOOKING ASWAN FROM THE WEST.*

118-119 *THE TOMBS OF THE GOVERNORS AT THE SITE OF QUBBET AL-HAWA ARE OVERLOOKED BY THE 'DOME OF THE WINDS,' A MUSLIM MAUSOLEUM THAT HAS GIVEN ITS NAME TO THE WHOLE HILL.*

119 BOTTOM LEFT *SARENPUT I, GOVERNOR AND SUPERINTENDENT OF THE PRIESTS OF SATET, IS PORTRAYED IN FRONT OF THE ENTRANCE TO HIS BURIAL PLACE.*

119 BOTTOM RIGHT *THIS FRAGMENTED STATUE PORTRAYING THE DECEASED COMES FROM THE TOMB OF SARENPUT II.*

PHILAE ISLAND

120-121 *The temple of the goddess Isis today stands on Agilkia Island.*

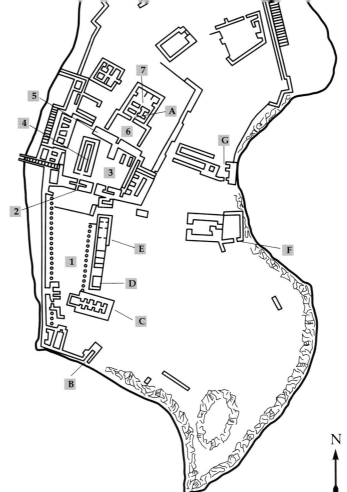

P hilae Island, which features a large temple dedicated to the goddess Isis, bride of Osiris and mother of Horus, is located south of Aswan, below the First Cataract. The decision to erect a temple in honor of the goddess here was probably due to the fact that the island was near that of Biga. There, it was believed, the body of Osiris rested and from there originated the waters that flooded Egypt, arising in turn from the humors exuded by the cadaver of the god.

Philae's most ancient monuments date back to the reign of Nectanebo I (380-362 B.C.) of the Thirtieth Dynasty who had a gate and a kiosk built for the goddess Isis, probably on the site of a more ancient structure of which no trace remains. In about 250 B.C., Ptolemy II Philadelphus transformed the temple was into a large cult center, around which rose other buildings. The island's landing-place was located in the southern part, not far from the kiosk of Nectanebo I; then the pious proceeded along two porticoes that led to the temple.

Once past the first pylon, a big courtyard was entered, at the back of which was the second pylon. On the western side of the courtyard was a *mammisi* (birth house), inside which Isis gave birth to her son Horus, with whom the pharaohs of Egypt were identified. The decorations of this building feature scenes relating to the birth of Horus. On the eastern side of the courtyard, a columned portico accommodating six small rooms was built. The one nearest the pylon contains the stairs that lead to the roof of the temple, where some cult chapels honoring Osiris are found. Adjacent to the first courtyard, a chapel dedicated to the Nubian god Mandulis (probably the work of the Roman conqueror Augustus) is found.

Beyond the second pylon (a full 72 feet tall and 125 feet wide), there is a room (or a hypostyle atrium) with ten columns, originally painted in lively colors. The ceiling of the room contains illustrations of an astrological nature: crafts navigating the sky and the repertory of the hours that correspond to the various stages along the path of the sun. This room leads to the *sanctum sanctorum,* where the statue of the resident divinity of the temple was kept.

Ptolemy II restored Nectanebo I's kiosk and also built a small *sacellum* (freestanding chapel within a temple) in honor of Imhotep, the patron deity of medicine. Ptolemy V and the Meroitic king Arkamani erected a place of worship for Arensnuphis, a Nubian god, opposite Nectanebo's gazebo. In the eastern part of the island, there is a small temple, built by Ptolemy II and dedicated to the goddess Hathor, who, infuriated had left Egypt and in the form of a lioness had spread devastation as far as Nubia. Once her rage was placated, the goddess stopped on Philae, where she assumed the role of the Lady of Joy. The entrance courtyard columns of this building have scenes relating to the myth of the goddess, among them some figures of instrumentalists or the dwarf god Bes, who beats a tambourine or plays the harp to pacify the goddess.

PHILAE ISLAND

122 TOP ON THE LEFT OF THE COURTYARD, THE 'BIRTH HOUSE,' OR MAMMISI, CAN BE SEEN.

122 BOTTOM IN THE GROOVE THAT OPENS ON THE FIRST PYLON, ONE OF THE VERY TALL POLES USED TO HOLD FLAGS WAS SET.

122-123 THE FIRST PYLON WAS ERECTED BY PTOLEMY XII.

123 TOP THE PHARAOH PRESENTS A POT OF INCENSE TO THE GODDESS ISIS.

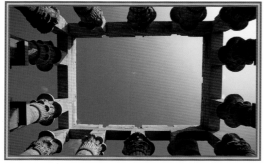

At the farthest point of the island's eastern coast is a gorgeous kiosk built during Emperor Trajan's reign (98-117 A.D.). It must be remembered that after the conquest of Egypt by Rome, Philae became the last stronghold of the religion of the Egypt of the pharaohs. On the island, the most recent hieroglyphic inscription found dates back to A.D. 394, and a few even more recent reliefs were found in Demotic, the latest of which is from A.D. 432. Even after Christianity had finally spread almost everywhere, the Egyptian priests of Philae continued to observe their ancient rituals. Nonetheless, in A.D. 535, the Byzantine emperor Justinian ordered that the temple be permanently closed. The temple priests and scribes were treated badly and the Christians, once having broken into the building, to the best if their ability obliterated the images of the gods and kings of Egypt. Philae then became a city inhabited by Coptic Christians; the site was surrounded by a wall and endowed with several churches, four of which were created out of the atrium of the temple of Isis and in the temples of Imhotep, Hathor, and Arensnuphis. The earliest dam at Aswan, built in 1898 and then raised in successive stages at the beginning of the twentieth century, resulted in the partial submersion of the temple: from December to June only the topmost parts of the building emerge from the water. Even though a boat tour among the capitals and pylons would be fascinating, the water was undoubtedly a threat to the survival of the buildings of Philae. A further threat presented itself in 1960, when the Sudanese government made the decision to build the second dam, which would have completely and permanently submerged the temple. Fortunately, in 1974, thanks to the intervention of the international community, the temples of Philae were dismantled stone by stone and later reconstructed on the small island of Agilkia, not far from Philae, but safe from the water. At the end of this colossal enterprise, thanks to Italian technicians, on March 10, 1980, the 'new' temple of Isis was finally inaugurated.

124 TOP THE KIOSK OF NECTANEBO I HAS PAPYRIFORM CAPITALS SURMOUNTED BY THE FACE OF HATHOR WITH COW EARS.

124 CENTER THE GAZEBO OF
TRAJAN WAS PROBABLY RELATED
TO RITES HELD WHEN THE
GODDESS ISIS LEFT THE ISLAND
DURING SACRED PROCESSIONS.

124 BOTTOM AND 124-125
THE KIOSK OF TRAJAN IS THE
MOST ELEGANT EXAMPLE OF
PERIPTERAL-TYPE EGYTPIAN
TEMPLES. THIS OPEN-FASCICLED
PAPYRIFORM CAPITAL IS
ILLUSTRATIVE OF ITS FINE
QUALITY.

125 BOTTOM FROM INSIDE THE
GREAT TEMPLE OF ISIS, THE
WATERS OF THE NILE CAN BE
GLIMPSED.

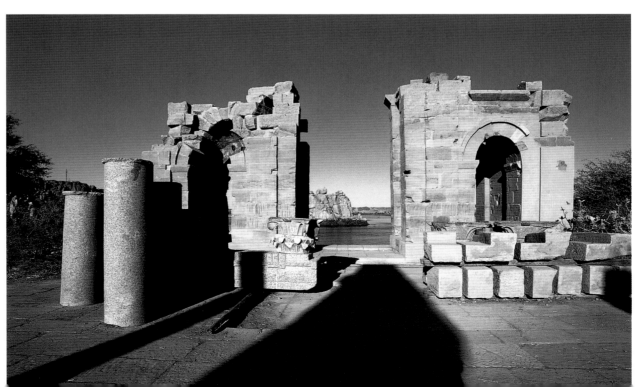

QERTASSI

The site of Qertassi contained a peripteral temple (i.e., with external columns) from the Greco-Roman era dedicated to the goddess Isis; it was saved from the waters of Lake Nasser and reassembled in 1963 near Aswan, 19 miles north of its original site. The building comprises a simple rectangular kiosk, surrounded by palm-shaped columns, with the intercolumns closed by partition walls that rise halfway up. Two columns, with capitals that portray the face of the goddess Hathor, flank the temple entrance.

126 TOP THIS STELA, LOCATED BETWEEN BEIT AL-WALI AND QERTASSI, CONTAINS THE CARTOUCHES OF THE 'KING OF UPPER AND LOWER EGYPT,' MEN-MAAT-RA, OR SETI I, FATHER OF THE GREAT RAMESSES II.

126 BOTTOM THE HATHORIC CAPITALS ARE COMPOSED OF THE FACE OF HATHOR, FEATURING THE CHARACTERISTIC COW EARS, AN ANIMAL SACRED TO THE GODDESS.

127 THE COLUMNS THAT FLANK THE TWO ENTRANCES TO THE TEMPLE ARE SURMOUNTED BY OPEN-FASCICLED HATHORIC CAPITALS.

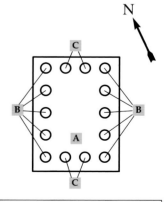

N

LEGEND

A PODIUM
B COLUMNS WITH PALM-SHAPED DESIGN
C PILLARS WITH HATHORIC CAPITALS

BEIT AL-WALI

About 28 miles south of the Aswan High Dam is the site of Beit al-Wali, now submerged by Lake Nasser. The site contained a rock temple built between about 1292 and 1290 B.C. by Ramesses II in honor of Amun-Ra of Thebes; it has now been moved to a site near the Aswan High Dam. Originally, a brick pylon stood in front of the temple. The layout of the building, dug into the rock, consists of an entrance atrium whose walls portray Ramesses' victories against the Libyans and Asians and the Nubians' presentation of tribute, including giraffes, monkeys, gold, and ivory tusks. From the atrium there is an entrance to a vestibule, which has two columns, and to the rear cella, or *sanctum sanctorum*. The scenes depicted on the walls of these last two rooms are of a religious nature.

128-129 THE KING SITS BETWEEN KHNUM AND ANUKIS IN THIS NICHE IN THE VESTIBULE.

128 BOTTOM THE TEMPLE OF BEIT EL-WALI MAY BE FOUNDED BETWEEN 1292 AND 1290 B.C. IN HONOR OF AMUN-RA OF THEBES.

129 TOP THE DOOR JAMS OF THE TEMPLE'S ACCESS PORTAL FEATURE RAMESSES II INTENT ON PERFORMING RITUAL GESTURES.

129 BOTTOM WITH HIS KHEPESH SWORD IN HAND, THE KING GRABS A PRISONER BY THE HAIR.

LEGEND

A ENTRANCE ATRIUM
B TWO-COLUMNED
    VESTIBULE
C CELLA

1 RAMESSES II, CONQUEROR OF THE LIBYANS AND ASIANS, AND THE PRESENTATION OF EXOTIC TRIBUTES BY THE NUBIANS

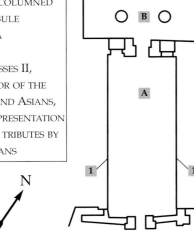

N

BEIT AL-WALI

130 *Prince Amunherunamef, son of Ramesses II, drags a few Syrian prisioners.*

131 *top Ramesses II is portrayed on a war chariot whose horse crashes into a formation of enemy soldiers.*

131 *bottom Ramesses II attacks a foreign fortress, from which fall some conquered enemies.*

KALABSHA

K alabsha, one of the most important cities of Lower Nubia and known to the ancient Egyptians as Taset and to the Greeks as Talmis, is found only a few miles south of Beit al-Wali. Here, Emperor Augustus ordered the construction of the biggest non-rock temple in Egyptian Nubia: 243 feet long and 108 feet wide, dedicated to the Nubian god Mandulis (identified with the Egyptian god Horus), who was flanked by the gods Osiris and Isis. The temple was surrounded by a wall and its entrance was formed by a pylon, through which a courtyard, a twelve-

columned hypostyle atrium, two vestibules, and finally, the rear cella were reached. Within the temple walls was a pre-exisitng chapel dedicated to the Nubian god Deduen and a second chapel most likely built by Ptolemy IX Soter II (116-107; restored 88-81 B.C.).

The temple was dismantled in 1962 - 63 and its numerous blocks moved and reassembled near the new dam at Aswan (New Kalabsha). Blocks from a grandiose Greco-Roman era entrance gate were found in the temple's foundations; this gate has since been rebuilt in the Egyptian Museum, Berlin.

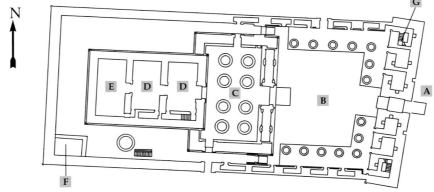

*132 TOP A WIDE PYLON GIVES
WAY TO THE TEMPLE OF
KALABSHA.*

*132 BOTTOM THE GOD KHNUM
COMES BEFORE ISIS IN THE
EXTERNAL RELIEFS OF THE
HYPOSTYLE ROOM.*

*132-133 THE PHOTO SHOWS THE
AREA IN WHICH THE TEMPLES OF
KALABSHA, QERTASSI, AND BEIT
AL-WALI STAND TODAY.*

N

LEGEND

A PYLON
B COURTYARD
C HYPOSTYLE ATRIUM
D VESTIBULE
E CELLA
F CHAPEL OF DEDUEN
G PTOLEMAIC CHAPEL

134-135 *The peristyle of the temple of Kalabsha, featuring columns along three sides, precedes the hypostyle room and, beyond that, the sanctuary.*

135 top *This detail of the lintel shows a typical symbol of royalty: a solar disk from which two cobras stick out,* one wearing the white crown of Upper Egypt and the other wearing the red crown of Lower Egypt.

136 *The bird with a human head is a representation of a spiritual element called* ba. *Here, a crown characteristic of a few divinities sits on its head.*

137 TOP *A TYPICAL PURIFICATION SCENE: HORUS, WITH A FALCON'S HEAD, AND THOTH, WITH AN IBIS'S HEAD, POUR WATER OVER THE HEAD OF THE SOVEREIGN.*

137 BOTTOM *THIS CAPITAL IN THE ATRIUM FEATURES TWO ROMAN INNOVATIONS: LITTLE VOLUTES AND A DESIGN WITH BUNCHES OF GRAPES AND VINE LEAFS.*

AL-DAKKA

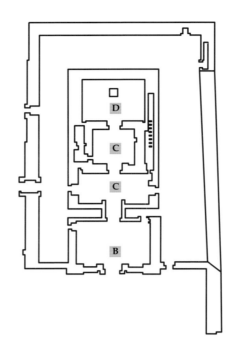

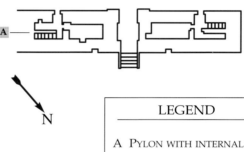

C alled Pselqet by the ancient Egyptians, al-Dakka contained a temple in honor of Thoth, god of writing and knowledge, often portrayed with a human body and the head of an ibis. Many rulers contributed to the temple's construction and decoration: they include the Meroïtic king Arkamani (early 3rd century B.C.), the Egyptian pharaohs Ptolemy IV Philopator (222-205 B.C.) and Ptolemy VIII Euergetes (170-163 and 145-116 B.C.), and the Roman emperors Augustus and Tiberius. The temple consisted of a big, stone pylon beyond which stood an atrium (transformed into a church during the Christian era), two vestibules, and a cella.

Between 1962 and 1968, the temple was dismantled and moved 25 miles further south, near Amada. During the dismantling project, a few blocks from a more ancient temple dating back to the Eighteenth Dynasty were excavated. This temple was dedicated to Horus of Baki (Quban), a site in Lower Nubia where a Middle-Kingdom fort stood.

LEGEND

A PYLON WITH INTERNAL STAIRCASES
B ATRIUM
C ATRIUM
D CELLA

138 TOP THE FAÇADE OF THE TEMPLE OF THOTH FEATURES FRAGMENTS OF RELIEFS BEARING RELIGIOUS SCENES REQUESTED BY PTOLEMY VIII EUERGETES II.

138 BOTTOM IN EACH OF THE TWO TOWERS ON THE PYLON, A STAIRCASE LEADS FROM A GROUND-FLOOR ROOM (THE PHOTOGRAPH SHOWS THEIR ENTRANCES) TO ANOTHER TWO UPPER-FLOOR ROOMS AND THE ROOF TERRACE.

138-139 THIS IS HOW THE TEMPLE OF DAKKA APPEARS TODAY, AT THE SITE WHERE IT WAS REBUILT AFTER ITS RESCUE FROM THE WATERS OF LAKE NASSER.

*139 BOTTOM DURING THE LAST
CENTURIES OF PAGANISM, THE
TEMPLE OF THOTH WAS ALSO
FREQUENTED BY NUMEROUS
VISITORS WHO LEFT BEHIND
INSCRIPTIONS IN DEMOTIC,
GREEK, AND MEROITIC.*

*140 TOP THE SOVEREIGN BRINGS
AN OFFERING TO THE GOD
HORUS, WITH A FALCON'S HEAD.*

*140-141 EMPEROR OCTAVIAN
AUGUSTUS, ADORNED WITH THE
EMBLEMS OF EGYPTIAN ROYALTY,
HOLDS OUT AN IMAGE OF MAAT
IN OFFERING.*

*141 TOP PTOLEMY VIII
EUERGETES II MAKES OFFERINGS
TO OSIRIS AND ISIS.*

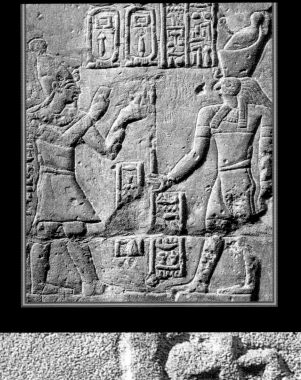

WADI ES-SEBUA

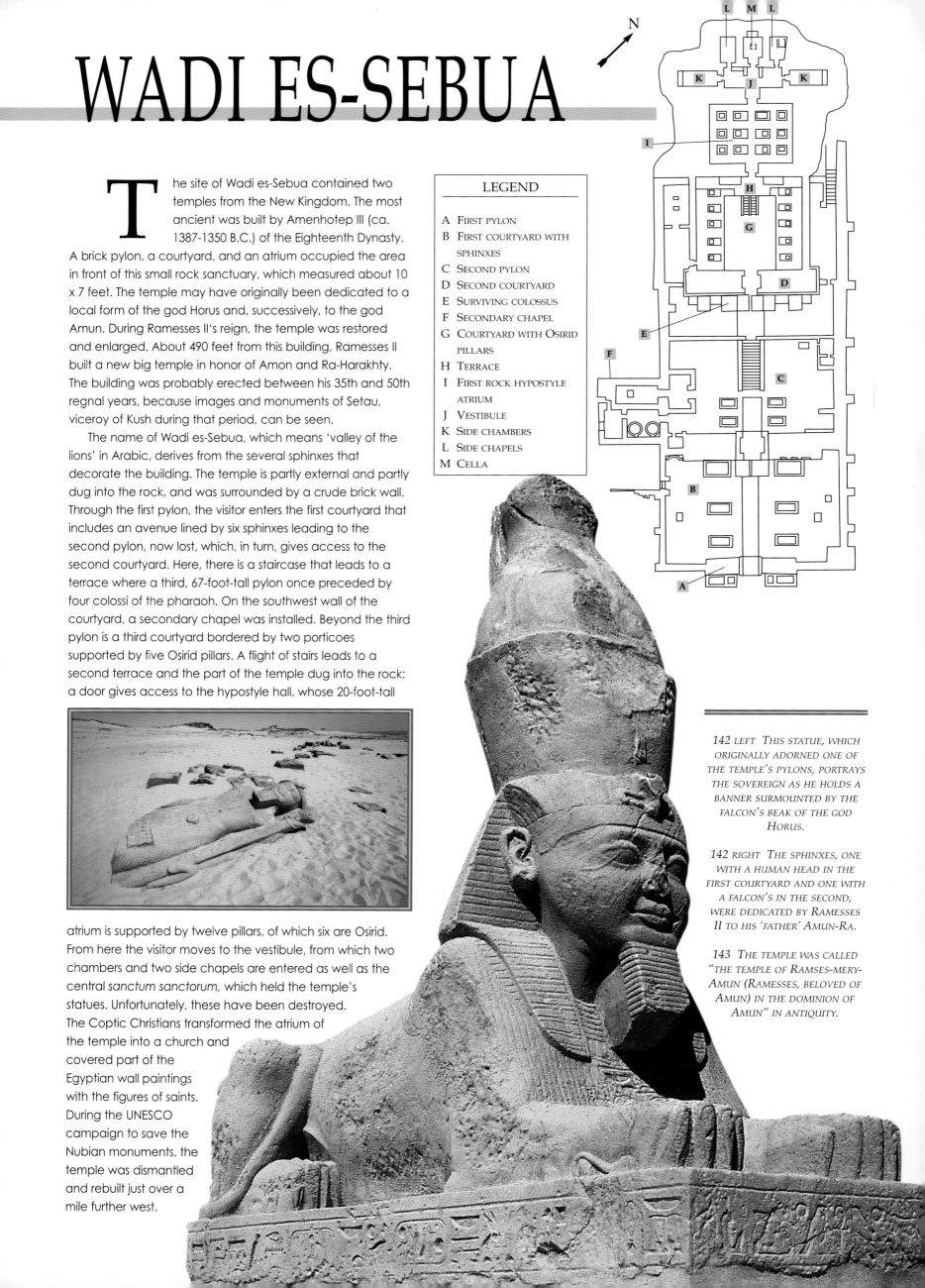

The site of Wadi es-Sebua contained two temples from the New Kingdom. The most ancient was built by Amenhotep III (ca. 1387-1350 B.C.) of the Eighteenth Dynasty. A brick pylon, a courtyard, and an atrium occupied the area in front of this small rock sanctuary, which measured about 10 x 7 feet. The temple may have originally been dedicated to a local form of the god Horus and, successively, to the god Amun. During Ramesses II's reign, the temple was restored and enlarged. About 490 feet from this building, Ramesses II built a new big temple in honor of Amon and Ra-Harakhty. The building was probably erected between his 35th and 50th regnal years, because images and monuments of Setau, viceroy of Kush during that period, can be seen.

The name of Wadi es-Sebua, which means 'valley of the lions' in Arabic, derives from the several sphinxes that decorate the building. The temple is partly external and partly dug into the rock, and was surrounded by a crude brick wall. Through the first pylon, the visitor enters the first courtyard that includes an avenue lined by six sphinxes leading to the second pylon, now lost, which, in turn, gives access to the second courtyard. Here, there is a staircase that leads to a terrace where a third, 67-foot-tall pylon once preceded by four colossi of the pharaoh. On the southwest wall of the courtyard, a secondary chapel was installed. Beyond the third pylon is a third courtyard bordered by two porticoes supported by five Osirid pillars. A flight of stairs leads to a second terrace and the part of the temple dug into the rock: a door gives access to the hypostyle hall, whose 20-foot-tall

atrium is supported by twelve pillars, of which six are Osirid. From here the visitor moves to the vestibule, from which two chambers and two side chapels are entered as well as the central *sanctum sanctorum*, which held the temple's statues. Unfortunately, these have been destroyed. The Coptic Christians transformed the atrium of the temple into a church and covered part of the Egyptian wall paintings with the figures of saints. During the UNESCO campaign to save the Nubian monuments, the temple was dismantled and rebuilt just over a mile further west.

LEGEND

A FIRST PYLON
B FIRST COURTYARD WITH SPHINXES
C SECOND PYLON
D SECOND COURTYARD
E SURVIVING COLOSSUS
F SECONDARY CHAPEL
G COURTYARD WITH OSIRID PILLARS
H TERRACE
I FIRST ROCK HYPOSTYLE ATRIUM
J VESTIBULE
K SIDE CHAMBERS
L SIDE CHAPELS
M CELLA

142 LEFT THIS STATUE, WHICH ORIGINALLY ADORNED ONE OF THE TEMPLE'S PYLONS, PORTRAYS THE SOVEREIGN AS HE HOLDS A BANNER SURMOUNTED BY THE FALCON'S BEAK OF THE GOD HORUS.

142 RIGHT THE SPHINXES, ONE WITH A HUMAN HEAD IN THE FIRST COURTYARD AND ONE WITH A FALCON'S IN THE SECOND, WERE DEDICATED BY RAMESSES II TO HIS 'FATHER' AMUN-RA.

143 THE TEMPLE WAS CALLED "THE TEMPLE OF RAMSES-MERY-AMUN (RAMESSES, BELOVED OF AMUN) IN THE DOMINION OF AMUN" IN ANTIQUITY.

144-145 The second pylon features a statue of Ramesses II bearing a standard. One of the four simulacra that stood by it has fallen, but it is still on site.

144 bottom The stone entrance gate is flanked by two statues of Ramesses II.

145 On the statue to the side of the entrance to the second pylon, the standard holds up a ram's head, an animal sacred to the god Amun.

146-147 Lake Nasser provides the background to the avenue of the sphinxes at the temple of Wadi es-Sebua.

AL-MAHARRAQA

Just south of al-Dakka is al-Maharraqa, built on the site of the ancient Hierasykaminos, a rather populous city of the Greco-Roman era. Hierasykaminos had a Roman-era temple dedicated to Serapis. Pharaoh Ptolemy I introduced this divinity into Egypt, perhaps with the intention of creating a cult that would be shared by both the Egyptians and the Greeks of Egypt. Serapis, whose name is the combination of that of two ancient Egyptian gods (Osiris and Hapy), was a god of the afterlife but also a physician

and therefore a benefactor of humanity. He borrowed some characteristics from Osiris, even if his main attributes were Greek, being those of Zeus, Aesculapius, and Dionysus.

The remains of temple of al-Maharraqa were limited to the hypostyle hall, which has porticoes on three sides; however, there is also a spiral staircase, the only example of this form in all of Nubia. In 1965-1966, the temple, threatened by the waters of Lake Nasser, was dismantled and rebuilt 19 miles further south of its original site, close to Wadi es-Sebua.

148 TOP LEFT THE ONLY SURVIVING ROOM OF THE TEMPLE IS THE HYPOSTYLE ROOM, WHICH FEATURES A PORTICO ON THREE SIDES.

148 TOP RIGHT THE PHOTOGRAPH SHOWS THE TOP OF THE TEMPLE OF MAHARRAQA AND, IN THE BACKGROUND, THAT OF DAKKA DEDICATED TO THOTH.

148 BOTTOM THE TEMPLE OF MAHARRAQA, THE ONLY ONE OF ITS KIND IN ALL OF NUBIA, HAS A SPIRAL STAIRCASE THAT LEADS TO THE TERRACE.

149 KEPT TO A BASIC FORM, THE TEMPLE OF SERAPIS AT MAHARRAQA WAS MOVED TO ITS PRESENT-DAY SITE BETWEEN 1965 AND 1966.

AMADA

Thutmosis III (Eighteenth Dynasty) ordered construction of temple of Amada in honor of Amun-Ra and Ra-Harakhty. Building was finished during the reign of his successor Amenhotep II (ca. 1450-1419 B.C.), then his successor, Thutmosis IV (ca. 1419-1386 B.C.), enlarged the temple. During the reign of the so-called 'heretic pharaoh' Akhenaten (ca. 1349-1334 B.C.), who sought to install the cult of Aten as Egypt's one and only god, the images of Amun were damaged. During the Nineteenth Dynasty, Seti I (ca. 1291-1278 B.C.) and Ramesses II intervened yet again in the temple with restorations and the enrichment of the decorations.

The temple's entrance is composed of a stone gateway, behind which there was originally a courtyard, closed on its sides by a brick wall and in the back by a portico with four columns. Later, Thutmosis IV transformed the courtyard into a stone atrium with its ceiling supported by four squared pillars. The vestibule and the cella with its side chapels are entered through the atrium. The reliefs that adorn the temple are of a religious nature; nonetheless, the building has two important historical inscriptions. The most ancient is dated the third year of Amenhotep II's reign and is engraved on a stela in the rear of the cella. It records a military campaign that the king undertook in Syria, which ended in the capture of seven enemy princes, who, as the inscription reports, were then "hung upside down from the bow of the boat of His Majesty." The other text is engraved on a stela placed on

150-151 *The temple of Amada was dedicated to the gods Amun of Thebes and Ra-Harakhty of Heliopolis.*

151 *top The god Ra-Harakhty holds Amenhotep II by the hand in a gesture of spiritual unity.*

151 *bottom King Thutmosis III holds out an ankh, the symbol of life, to a divinity.*

LEGEND

A STONE PORTAL
B ATRIUM OF THUTMOSIS IV
C VESTIBULE
D SIDE CHAPELS
E CELLA

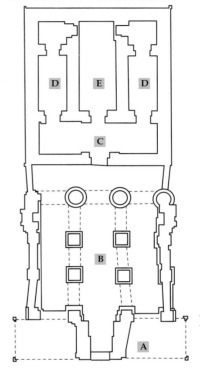

N

the left side of the entrance door; it tells of the defeat of the Libyans in an attempted invasion of Egypt during the fourth year of the reign of Merenptah (ca. 1212-1202 B.C.), Ramesses II's successor.

Like the other Egyptian and Nubian temples, that of Amada was also transformed into a church during the Christian era.

Between late 1964 and early 1975, the temple was removed from Lake Nasser to a safe site about a mile and a half distant and 213 feet up. A part of the temple, which weighed about 990 tons, was transferred in one piece: a steel-and-cement harness absorbed the bumps and vibrations while the monument was lifted, placed on wheels, and moved.

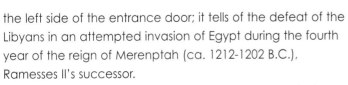

AL-DERR

A l-Derr had a rock temple dedicated by Ramesses II to the gods Ra-Harakhty and Amun-Ra. The layout of the building is rather simple and recalls that of the big temple at Abu Simbel. The first atrium, divided into five naves with twelve squared pillars and walls that feature battle scenes against the Nubians, gives access to a second atrium with a ceiling supported by six squared pillars. The walls of this atrium have reliefs of a religious nature, in which the pharaoh performs rituals and makes offerings in the presence of various divinities, among them the deified Ramesses II himself.

From here, the visitor moves on to the central cella that held the sitting statues of the divinities worshipped in the sanctuary: Ra-Harakhty, the selfsame Ramesses II, Amun-Ra of Thebes, and Ptah of Memphis. The central cella is flanked by two side chapels. In 1964, the temple was dismantled and rebuilt seven miles farther north, near the site of Amada. Today, the first atrium is recognizable only from the remains of the pillars; nevertheless, the rest of the building is in decent condition and it is possible to recognize the mutilated statues and the modifications made by the Copts who transformed the building into a Christian church.

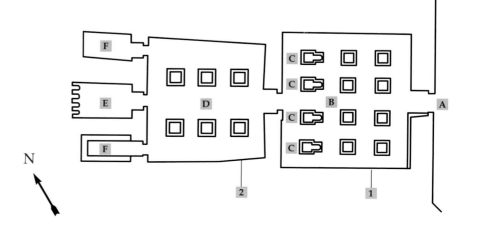

LEGEND

A ENTRANCE
B FIRST ATRIUM
C OSIRIDE PILLARS
D SECOND ATRIUM
E CELLA WITH FOUR STATUES
F SIDE CHAPELS

1 BATTLING THE NUBIANS
2 THE KING OFFICIATING
    AND MAKING OFFERINGS

152 RAMESSES II IS WELCOMED
WITH AN EMBRACE BY
RA-HARAKHTY.

152-153 IN THE BACK OF THE
FIRST HYPOSTYLE ROOM IN THE
TEMPLE OF DERR, THE ORIGINAL
OSIRID PILLARS HAVE BEEN
PARTIALLY PRESERVED.

153 bottom RAMESSES II
PLACES FLOWERS ON THE SACRED
BOAT OF RA-HARAKHTY.

154-155 *IN THE RELIEFS OF THE*
SECOND ATRIUM, RAMESSES II
CARRIES OUT RITUALS IN HONOR
OF SEVERAL DIVINITIES.

155 *TOP THE SCENES AND TEXTS*
IN THE SECOND ATRIUM ARE OF A
RELIGIOUS NATURE.

155 *BOTTOM RAMESSES II OFFERS*
TWO SMALL JUGS OF WINE TO
AMUN-RA.

A niba, called Mi'am by the Ancient Egyptians, stood on the Nile's west bank. During the New Kingdom, the city became the administrative center of Wawat (Lower Nubia) and its importance grew.

Aniba had a fort, probably erected during the Middle Kingdom and later enlarged during the New Kingdom, and a temple of Horus of Mi'am, founded by Senusret I (Twelfth Dynasty) and later restructured during the Eighteenth Dynasty.

Around the city were numerous necropolises from several eras, with constructed or rock-hewn tombs. One of these tombs is perhaps the most important monument in Aniba. It

OF PENNUT

156-157 In the atrium of the tomb of Pennut, the niche contains three unfinished statues of divinities.

156 bottom The tomb of Pennut was dug into a hill and rebuilt in the area of

Amada in order to save it from the waters of Lake Nasser.

157 bottom left and right The final scenes in the decorations of the tomb depict the interment of the official.

is the tomb of Pennut, governor of Uauat and superintendent of the temple of Horus of Mi'am during the reign of Ramesses VI (ca. 1141-1133 B.C.) The wife of Pennut, named Takha, performed the tasks of a 'singer' inside the local temple.

The tomb of Pennut is dug into the rock and has a cruciform layout. Beyond the entrance is an atrium in whose floor, between the entrance and the rear cella, is the burial chamber well. The walls of this room are entirely covered with reliefs that depict important events in Pennut's life, such as his dedication of a statue of Ramesses VI at the temple of al-Derr, or moments that describe funeral rituals or Pennut's survival in the hereafter. For example, the god Anubis can be seen standing next to Pennut's sarcophagus, while the goddess Isis, dressed in white, and Nephtys, dressed in red, lament his death with their arms raised in desperation. And then there is a fine image of Horus leading Pennut and his wife into the presence of Osiris, lord of the afterlife, who is sitting on a throne behind which stand the goddesses Isis and Neftis. From the atrium, the visitor moves to the rear cella, which has three unfinished statues of divinities sculpted into the living rock. The tomb of Pennut, fortunately, was saved from the rising waters and rebuilt 25 miles northeast of its original site, near Amada.

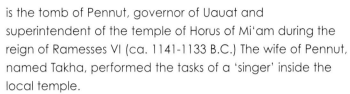

INDEX

PHOTO CREDITS

160
*THE NIGHT IS VANQUISHED BY
THE LIGHT IN A PHOTOGRAPH OF
THE GREAT TEMPLE OF ABU
SIMBEL. EVEN RAMESSES THE
GREAT MIGHT HAVE
APPRECIATED SUCH A MAJESTIC
AND EVOCATIVE SPECTACLE.*